They All Want to Write

Alvina Treut Burrows

June D. Ferebee

Doris C. Jackson

Dorothy O. Saunders

They All Want to Write

WRITTEN ENGLISH
IN THE
ELEMENTARY SCHOOL

Prentice-Hall, Inc.   New York   1952

PRENTICE-HALL EDUCATION SERIES

Harold Spears, Editor

PN
171
.C5
B8

Foreword

THE current emphasis on creative writing is a result of a number of related developments in modern education. One of these grows out of the widespread conviction that the primary aim of education is to assist in the development of well-oriented and reasonably well-adjusted young people. Some educational leaders believe that this goal can be attained only by incorporating creative activities in a broad educational program that seeks to offset some of the influences of a technological world. This point of view is endorsed by psychiatrists and psychologists. Both groups direct attention to the basic needs of the child and assert that the curriculum should be built with a primary concern for their fulfillment. One need that is generally mentioned relates to wholesome physical and mental development. Psychologists point out that the normal healthy child is one who is active and spontaneously alive; as he grows older, the persistence of spontaneity and creativity will reflect continuous, wholesome growth.

Was there ever a time when it seemed so imperative that our

v

schools assume a special responsibility for safeguarding the mental health of boys and girls? To do so it is essential to provide and maintain atmospheres for learning that foster spontaneity and creativity, and to offer children recognition, security, and happiness. Release, expression, and continuous growth will surely follow.

To provide escape and self-expression is one important function of creative writing, but there are others that, from the standpoint of mental health, are similarly significant. Creative writing may be so conceived and developed that it will serve a three-fold function, enabling each child to record his significant experiences and to share his activities and interests as well as to express himself freely, spontaneously, and joyously. To serve these ends creative writing must be thought of as composition in which the child is free to select his subject matter and to determine the length and form in which his writing will appear. Conceived in this way, creative writing will not be confined to poetry or any other form of expression; nor will it be considered the prerogative of gifted children.

During the past decade, many teachers have sought to foster creative writing in the classroom. And a number of professional books that emphasize the significance of creative writing have appeared during this period. The writers of some of these books stressed the importance of individual expression; yet they appeared to be interested primarily in the form, rather than in the content, of children's writing.

Another group of writers also emphasized the importance of personal reaction and individual expression; but they considered creative expression as a *means,* rather than an *end,* of instruction. They recommended that creative products be appraised by considering the extent to which they mirror the genuine reaction and expression of the pupil. This point of view was strongly endorsed by progressively minded teachers everywhere. In fact, just prior to World War II, several books appeared in which teachers themselves presented creative writing as a living, vital form of communication. One of the most significant of these volumes was *They All Want to Write,* in which four teachers described work in one school. They discussed two types of writing, the personal and the practical. In personal writing, all factors that hinder free expression were discouraged. . . "It is getting down in one's own language what one thinks or feels that is important." The second type of writing, to be read by another, "should be as clear as it can be made. The notice, the business letter, the report to be given to the teacher or to be filed as reference material must, therefore, meet high standards of clarity, correctness, and arrangement." In this type of writing, errors were sought and corrected; then the final product was carefully copied.

The revision, like the earlier book, will prove genuinely helpful to many classroom teachers, since it records the steps teachers have actually followed in fostering creative writing. And it sets forth the results in the form of children's own compositions. Moreover, this volume brings out more clearly than any other the fact that creative writing offers an excellent vehicle for recognizing, respecting, and cultivating individuality. Chapter 6, "Individual Differences in Writing," presents seven case studies and gives a clear picture of the varied development of each child through samples of his personal and practical writing. Herein we find the developmental concept of education in operation. Education is viewed as a process that aims to bring about the maximum development of each child in terms of his unique nature and needs. As each picture unfolds, we also perceive the role of the teacher. We note the recognition of, and concern for, each child's many-sided nature, and for his attitudes and values. We observe also the contributions that different teachers make by working cooperatively to promote the continuous growth of each child.

It is the hope of the writer that the revised edition of a remarkable volume will be read by a new generation of teachers whose understanding and appreciation of the art of teaching will be equaled only by their enhanced regard for children and their responsibility for fostering growth through creative expression.

PAUL WITTY

We discover, too, what seems to be a law of the creative spirit, that it does not, except on rare occasions, give forth its best at once. — HUGHES MEARNS, Creative Youth

That problem is to direct pupils' oral and written speech, used primarily for practical and social ends, so that gradually it shall become a conscious tool of conveying knowledge and assisting thought. — JOHN DEWEY, How We Think

Preface

They All Want to Write was first published in 1939 as a record of our experience in helping children learn to write. About one hundred children formed the core of our study, some sixty of whom we handled over a period of four years. They were organized as follows:

Group I	*Group II*
31 children	30 children
Grades 3 and 4 — Saunders	Grades 3 and 4 — Jackson
Grades 5 and 6 — (Treut) Burrows	Grades 5 and 6 — Ferebee

Group III	*Group IV*
31 children	20 children
Grades 3 and 4 — Saunders	Grades 1 and 2 — Jackson

The teaching of writing was but one aspect of our work, for as grade teachers we were responsible for the social adjustments of our groups and for their achievement in all areas of subject matter.

This revised edition of *They All Want to Write* reports the growth in understanding and the development of techniques that have come about in thirteen years of further experience with children and their writing.

Those chapters devoted to teaching procedures — "First Steps in Writing," "Practical Writing," and "Personal Writing" — have been completely re-organized and re-written in order to expand and enrich the presentation of our writing program. Two important new sections have been added: "Children's Verse" and "Story Supplement."

Since our basic philosophy has remained essentially unchanged, the chapters entitled "Children and Writing" and "The Long View" have been but slightly altered. Chapter 6, also, is without major changes, for the seven case studies reported there have lost none of their value as descriptions of growth.

We hope that this new book will give a clear and useful picture of our way of teaching children to write.

As we have continued to study and to experiment we have grown increasingly aware of our debt to Hughes Mearns. He stood with us at the fork of the road, and he turned our steps into a new way — a way whose signpost read: "This path leads to a heightened respect for each individual and an abiding faith in his innate power." It is because we followed where Hughes Mearns led that the substance of this book came to be.

Our gratitude goes also to J. Ralph McGaughy, who was our guide and stay in bringing the first edition through to publication.

THE AUTHORS

Acknowledgments

EXCERPTS are reprinted in this volume from the following books by special permission of, and arrangement with, the original publishers or authors: *How We Think,* by John Dewey, D. C. Health and Company; *Creative Youth,* by Hughes Mearns, Doubleday & Company, Inc., and Hughes Mearns; *The Prophet,* by Kahlil Gibran, Alfred A. Knopf, Inc.; *Come Hither,* by Walter de la Mare, MCA Managment, Ltd.; *The Art of Thinking* and *What We Live By,* by E. Dimnet, and *A Philosophy of Solitude,* by John Cowper Powys, Simon and Schuster, Inc.; *From the South Seas,* by Margaret Mead, William Morrow & Company, Inc.; *Home Book of Quotations,* by Egbert Burton Stevenson, Dodd, Mead and Company, Inc.; *Letters of John Keats to His Family and Friends,* edited by Sidney Colvin, The Macmillan Company, 1925.

Contents

The teacher who walks in the shadow of the temple, among his followers, gives not of his wisdom but rather of his faith and his lovingness.

If he is indeed wise he does not bid you enter the house of his wisdom, but rather leads you to the threshold of your own mind. — KAHLIL GIBRAN, The Prophet

1. Children and Writing

*W*E believe that writing can play a significant part in a child's development. For that reason we have sought a way to release freer, more genuine self-expression and at the same time to cultivate the skill necessary for writing with correctness and ease. All who have worked with children know the deep-rooted antagonism of these two aims. Our early experiments to accomplish both were so discouraging that we questioned whether it were possible to make a child the minstrel of his own free spirit and a careful scribe as well. But in time we found a way, which has given during each succeeding year a better and more abundant return. We have become clearly certain that this concept of writing brings children deep personal satisfaction as well as effective control of its essential mechanics.

We know that if a child is to be an effective, poised personality, he must have an awareness and an appreciation of his own power. Such self-knowledge comes only through frequent

1

opportunity to experiment and to fumble along the lines of his desire until out of his effort he fashions something which in his eyes is good. That the product is often crude and clumsy does not matter. The important thing is that the child, out of himself and working in his own way, has produced a thing of which he can approve. The satisfaction he has had in what he has made — that momentary kinship with creative power — makes him seem worthy to himself. And once having tasted such deep delight, he rarely rests content, but tries again and again, spurred on by those exhilarating moments when the excitement of creating possesses him.

THE DISTINCTION BETWEEN PRACTICAL AND PERSONAL WRITING

Many kinds of experience offer opportunity for such self-expression, and writing is one of those most commonly available. We recognize that there are two fundamental kinds of writing. One is practical, the other personal. There is a gratifying sense of power that comes to any individual when he can fulfill the practical writing demands of his own life, whether it be the first brief direction that goes home from school or the lengthy treatise that terminates an original study. And even more telling in its expansive effect is the personal writing that wells up out of the depths of the spirit.

Through our experience we learned that these two kinds of writing must be handled differently. We have given ample training in utilitarian writing, and we have encouraged personal writing for the sheer fun of doing it.

We began by accepting generously and sincerely whatever personal writing was given, no matter how poor it might be. This was not always easy, for sometimes the offering was very bad, and the urge and impatience for improvement were strong within us. However, we bit our tongues and remembered that first of all we must have children writing freely and without anxiety. Until this was accomplished, all else must wait.

As the children came to know that we accepted their personal expression in the form it came to us, and that we did not want to make it over to suit our standards, free writing periods became transformed. Immediately the impulse to write grew stronger, and the volume rapidly increased. Often in the morning a child came to the teacher's desk with this remark: "Gee, I have a swell idea. Will we have time to write to-day?" Sometimes cronies got together, each with a story to share, or a group clustered about a desk listening to the latest adventure of Chimino or The Five Bears. To have to stimulate writing had ceased to be one of our tasks. In fact, as momentum grew, we seemed to be regarded as casual members of the group. The children, unconfused by coercion or arbitrary direction, wrote only to what we think should be the normal and honest purposes of all such writing: Each strove to please himself or to entertain others; and the degree to which he felt he fulfilled his purpose determined the quality of his satisfaction. He wrote because he wanted to put his own interesting idea into words; he wanted his story to delight the crowd, to catch their interest with its first phrase, to move before them like a living picture, to make them laugh or hold their breath.

TEACHING PRINCIPLES

Ever since we began expecting children to write only when they had a genuine need or the earnest desire to do so, we have found them eager to write well. In that mood they have been sensitive to our guidance and suggestion. Whenever a child is writing to fulfill some practical purpose, we do not hesitate to offer such teaching and criticism as we think he can profitably use; but we do not tamper with an individual piece of personal writing. In that field our effort is directed toward building into the child's consciousness a realization of what makes writing good, and our usual method is through appreciating the good thing when it appears. The original idea, the fresh invention, or the vivid, individual way of saying a thing is singled out for glowing comment because we know the things approved determine the direction of growth. This is ordinarily done when the children are sharing their work with one another. As they grow increasingly aware of the elements of good writing, their spontaneous appreciation becomes more discriminating and concrete.

In time the teacher seems to sit most of the while in the background, just listening quietly. In reality she is still directing with utmost care, but she injects her guidance so unobtrusively that it does not arouse resistance nor disrupt the wholesome spirit of rapport. Even when an epidemic of gangster stories or stereotyped plots breaks out, she does not show dismay or waste her energy berating them. Instead, she watches closely for those flashes of good writing that always appear, knowing well that offensive things when ignored gradually drop away if there are better things to take their place. She takes occasion, also, to read more of other people's stories — tall tales, animal episodes, humorous everyday adventures — until she diverts their attention, and sometimes starts a counter-epidemic.

Under this way of working, personal writing is for our children a happy, spontaneous experience. Much of what they write is trivial, but at times we are startled by the power they reveal. Disarmed by the disguise of fictitious character and incident, they divulge secret yearnings and resentments that they would never consciously betray; for childhood appears to be an alien land in which grown-up behavior is frankly appraised according to its immediate effect upon the children themselves. This is a point of view that adults rarely encounter because boys and girls, for their own protection, have learned to conceal it. When they are writing freely out of their inmost selves, however, it is bound to be exposed, and we have had to be ready to hear the truth as they see it. Only by detached acceptance of their real feelings can we get the sincerity and vigor that we profess to crave.

Thus we have tried to preserve for each child the privilege of writing out of the depths of his own nature and in the rhythmic pattern peculiar to himself. We have held ourselves responsible for creating a schoolroom atmosphere in which he can express himself happily and abundantly without fear or strain. Through appreciative comment on attributes of good writing we have encouraged observation, invention, clear vivid expression, and honest individual flavor. And finally, at times quite apart from the writing periods, we have exposed them to good literature, which we have enjoyed in a friendly, unhurried fashion with time enough to see in our minds the pictures, and to chuckle or to "shiver in our boots" together.

Because it is difficult at best to catch on paper one's very own ideas, we frankly allow in personal writing the disregard of all factors that hinder. Spelling, penmanship, appearance are not considered; it is the getting down in one's own language what one thinks or feels that is important. The child does not write a paper to be looked at; he makes a purely personal recording to be shared or privately enjoyed as he may choose.

On the other hand, writing that is to be read by another, both because of courtesy and practicability, should be as clear as it can be made. Therefore, the notice, the business letter, the report must meet high standards of clarity, correctness, and arrangement. When they have seen real need for making an excellent final draft, most of our children have worked willingly over their practical writing until it represents the best that they can do. Different ways of expressing an idea and different forms of organization are experimented with until the most effective one is chosen. Mechanical errors are searched for and corrected, and, finally, the paper to be used is carefully transcribed, for the child knows that when he is making a draft to be used by others, his best craftsmanship is necessary.

Furthermore, we have found that those elements of good writing acquired in ways that have meaning to the child gradually fuse into an enlarged and strengthened writing power. Thus the absolute and fearless honesty of expression exercised in all personal writing gives color and conviction to his practical writing; and items of mechanics and sentence form learned in practical writing become matters of common use in what he writes for his own satisfaction. Through the elementary years our children have continued to write with eagerness and with increasing effectiveness. They find it fun to fix in words an evanescent, beautiful thought, or to make up a good story for their crowd; and they get no less pleasure from their ability to report factual material with aliveness and clarity. To have writing a joy instead of a drudgery is an experience still so unique that we think the way we have found is worthy of more detailed explanation.

The desire for writing grows with writing.
— ERASMUS, Adagio

2. Children Begin to Write

FOR weeks the first-grade group had been looking forward to their own picnic. Throughout the winter there had been parties, of course, but every single one of them had been planned for others. Now, at the end of the year, the long-promised time had come and the fun of doing something "just for us" was highly exciting. Naturally, the most important part of a picnic is what you have to eat. Interest in that discussion needed no boosting. When the kinds of sandwiches and fruit were agreed upon, we translated the menu into a store order, writing it on the blackboard for all to see. Three children were chosen to go to the local grocery and find prices that very day. Since first-grade children could not cross the streets alone when the traffic officer was absent, several sixth-grade boys were asked to go along. It would be difficult to say who were the more proud, the elder guides or the three young messengers! Each took his list, which he had copied from the board, and each recorded the prices given by the groceryman. One list is to be seen on page 7.

6

Harry

Price of 5 lb. 2 bananas @ 7¢ .35

3 lbs. butter @ 31¢ .93

6 sliced bread @ 10¢ .60

4 tomatoes @ 15¢ . .60

4 carrots @ 7¢ .28

3 oranges .07

1 pt. mayonaise .33

wax paper . 15

Grocery list for picnic. Written at end of first grade.

When the shoppers returned to school, the prices they brought were added to the order that was still on the board. The teacher found the total and did the necessary division. Every youngster watched closely to see how much money he would need to bring, and when the result was found wrote on a slip of paper: "I need 14 cents for the picnic."

This, of course, made it official. Mother could see that a bona fide request was being made. The slips were taken home at lunch time and that afternoon every single child brought his fourteen cents. Important matters are not likely to be forgotten even by six-year-olds!

Then the same three children who had gone on the morning errand went back to the store and bought the food. They took the same lists again and *used* them, this time as shopping memoranda. A few others went along to help carry packages. When they returned, everything was ready to begin the actual preparation of the picnic lunch.

During the process of washing carrots and making sandwiches, a child remarked: "You know, we ought to thank Miss Wetzel's children for taking us to the store."

"A fine idea," we agreed. "They did something very nice for us and we should thank them. Who wants to do it?"

A few volunteered. The letters were written almost immediately and sent to the older children who had been their guides during the morning. Facsimiles of two are included here. A third letter follows:

> DEAR MISS WETZEL'S CLASS,
>   Thank you for taking our children across
> the street. If three of our children went
> alone they would get run over by a car.
>   Love from
>   SAM

We doubt that the drawing up of a business contract is of more serious moment to an adult than the writing of the grocery

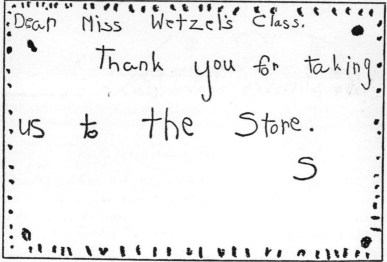

First grade letters of appreciation.

9

order was to these first-graders. The copying had to be exactly right; the success of the picnic depended on it. Through such concrete experiences our children come to know the practical value that writing can have in their own lives and to appreciate why it must be carefully done. Its results are often visible, or tangible, or even edible.

One of the early steps in letter writing.

BEGINNINGS OF COMPOSITION

In other ways, too, the child discovers that writing is useful in his daily living. He learns to write his name so that he can identify his own materials. He copies a word or phrase from the blackboard so that he will remember to bring his lunch money or his sneakers. Here are further suggestions for writing that is allied to a genuine need:

Signs on collections
Lists of children's names and telephone numbers
Lists of birds seen on bird walks
Daily temperature records

Memoranda concerning material to be brought from home for
    cooking
Captions for pictures or movies
Lists of supplies needed for making a terrarium
Calendars
Greeting cards for special holidays and birthdays
Signs to advertise money-raising campaigns

John
Time Note

Tues.	8:45	to	11:30
	2:00	to	3:00
Wed.	8:45	to	11:30
Thurs.	8:45	to	11:30
Fri.	8:45	to	10:00

*An illustration of the need for teacher assistance
in completing an important notice.*

As soon as the composition of ideas, no matter how simple,
enters into a writing experience, we talk about the ideas first.
At this time the children decide what they want to say and we
write it on the blackboard so that they may copy it. In October,
for instance, it is necessary to tell the parents the exact hours
of the new afternoon session. One class formulated and many
children copied the following message:

        We come at 1:00.
        We go at 2:30.

Each child carried his note home proudly because he was telling his mother something she needed to know.

Copying from the blackboard is hard work at first. Large-sized Manila paper without lines and fat pencils help to make this easier for beginning writers. Nevertheless, there are always some whose concentration and muscular skill are not sufficiently developed for them to do as much as the others. A great deal of encouragement needs to be given to these children so that their first faltering steps in writing will bring them satisfaction. Always we stand ready to give approval to those who are making a sincere effort, no matter how meager their accomplishments. Occasionally we do part of the writing as illustrated on page 11 or we excuse certain individuals from the task.

As time goes on, however, we make sure that even the slowest children write enough to grow in independence. Situations frequently arise when but one copy of a letter can be used. After the class has composed the message, we select a child who needs the additional practice to do the copying. Here is such a letter:

> To the School Store:
>   Please bring a large roll of brown
> paper to our room. We want to make a big
> picture. We are in Room 136.
>   Mrs. Jackson's Class

Donald was chosen to prepare the order. Having such a responsibility touched his pride and he set to work to do the best he could. Fortunately, he could write at his own slow tempo without the discouragement of being outstripped by more capable neighbors working at the same task. Finally, after considerable labor, he finished the order and delivered it to the school store. When the paper arrived, Donald obviously felt that he had done a good job. It is such satisfactions that compensate for struggling effort and spur a child on toward mastery.

When a piece of writing is finished, the children often put it up so that everyone has a chance to see it. Because they thoroughly enjoy looking at one another's work, the bulletin board receives careful inspection from all members of the class. Frequently, we talk with them about the good points in each

Jan., 18, 1950

Dear children,

It was very nice of you to give the class a ride.
I liked the ride very much and so did the other children
Thank you for giving Mrs. Jackson a ride.

Pat

*One of the first individually composed letters, dictated to the teacher
and completed by the child.*

13

paper, commenting upon neat arrangement, careful formation of letters, and appropriate illustrations. Taking time to enjoy what they have done offers immediate dividends for their investment of effort.

After many experiences in which the group makes up the message and the class copies it from the board, the children are ready to compose individually. There is the usual class discussion, when they talk over the main points to be included in their letters. Following this, each dictates his own message and the teacher writes it. Then the child puts in the date, the greeting, and the close. To make it more his own, he invariably adds some sort of decoration.

In the thank-you note on page 13, Pat, of course, decided what he wanted to say; his teacher typed it for him, and then he finished the job. Naturally the illustration was to him an important part of the message. The "Dear Children" were an older group in the school who had taken the first-graders on a sleighing party. Before many weeks Pat had sufficient muscular control to enable him to copy a whole letter including the dictated message.

In the daily life at school there are many opportunities for children to write messages that are important to them. A child may dictate a note to his mother asking for a smock or one to the science teacher inquiring how to set up an aquarium. Perhaps he helps others phrase a short letter to a neighboring group inviting them to inspect the new lighthouse just built in the classroom; or he helps to plan a class note requesting permission to go on a trip, and he makes a copy for Mother to sign. Sometimes he dictates a letter to Father "just for fun" — one that is brief enough for him to copy by himself and illustrate eloquently.

All possible variations of the telling-dictating-helping-copying procedure occur at this early age. At the same time the children continue to write the lists, labels, and memoranda that are needed to make their daily living go more smoothly. However, the amount of writing that can be expected in the first school year depends, of course, upon the children's emotional stability and their mental and physical maturity. Unquestionably we have found it wiser to expect too little rather than too much. Young children should not write so frequently or at such length that writing becomes a task they dread.

Milk   Bill   March   4

         through   May   3

7   weeks   at   22¢ - 154

Good   Friday
one   day   we   forgot } - .09
                                 ────
                               $ 1.45
                                paid

Child in charge of milk delivery submitted this bill. This experience was suffi-ciently meaningful to sustain his interest and effort.

BUILDING STANDARDS

In the notes and letters that our children write we take pains to stress the value of the individual touch. We call it "something in your letter that is just like you." We begin with the first copied notes by commenting on anything in the decoration that is unique or distinctive, and when letters are independently composed we transfer our attention to the ideas they express.

Dear Miss Stone,

Thank you very much for letting us have the butter churn. It made such nice butter It made such a funny noise when it was near the end We had a terrible hard time

pulling it up and down.

Love from Vicki

The individual reaction is encouraged

16

Dear Miss Stone,
    Thank you for the churn
I liked the butter it made

We had it on crackers. I
didn't know anything about how
to make butter because Mommie
never made it. She buys it

from the A+P

    from Ruth

in all writing experiences.

Dear   Miss   Greve,
            Thank   you
for   taking   the   chickens
home.   Did they   get   out

of   the   bath   tub?

            There   is   one

black   one   that   looks   like

he   has   a   flag   on

his   wing.

            How   can   they   sleep

standing   up?   I   should   think

they   would   fall   down.   I   get

so   tired   on   my   feet   that

I   do.   Love   from   Danny.

The personal flavor of this letter was sustained because the child was given the opportunity to dictate the final portion.

18

As a child holds up his finished work so that the class can see, we read it aloud, and someone — child or teacher — points out any parts that show the writer has done some personal thinking and feeling about what he has said. Thus in Vicki's thank-you note we commented on the way she described the butter churn: "It made such a funny noise when it was near the end. We had a terrible hard time pulling it up and down." And we enjoyed Ruth's quite different reaction, when she said, "I didn't know anything about how to make butter because Mommie never made it. She buys it from the A and P." This practice of hearing and seeing one another's work and appreciating its flavor greatly stimulates writing interest and growth.

Very gradually children acquire writing skills, which sooner or later enable them to dispense with the teacher-stenographer. Although they cannot spell all the words that they want to use, they ask for the ones they need, and they have the ability to hold a thought while putting it on paper. This transition from dictating and copying to the independent writing of each sentence as it is composed is a big step. Often, in order to preserve the all-important idea of "making it sound like you," we come to a child's aid by writing from dictation the final portion. Countless letters have been saved from commonplace endings by this device.

A letter is corrected by the child and teacher together. It may be copied if necessary. Not all writing requires more than one draft, but by the time a child arrives at the end of the third grade he has had a number of experiences where copying has been essential. This is usually due to the rapid and oftentimes untidy writing that results from trying to get ideas down before they are forgotten. Since children recognize the importance of having in "good shape" anything that is to be read by someone else, they accept the job of making a fresh copy.

The checking of first drafts affords opportunity to teach punctuation, such as commas after the salutation of a letter and between the numbers in the date, periods after the abbreviation of the name of a month and at the ends of sentences, and capitals

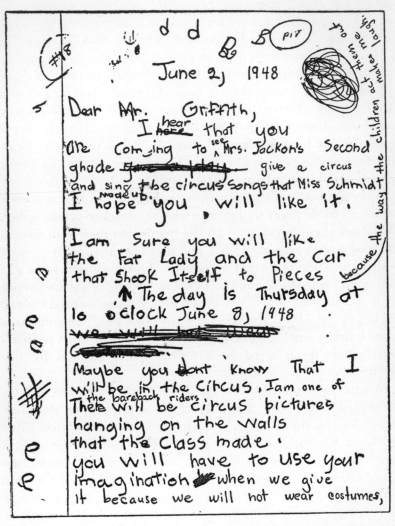

First draft, with concluding paragraph dictated to teacher. The whole letter

.I think the music
of ~~The~~ Bareback Rider   # 8
is ~~very sweet~~ yummy. It
makes me feel that I'm
a very wonderful person —
that I am walking in
the breeze up a hill.

~~Hese~~

)

was then checked by child and teacher together. Note content and fluency.

21

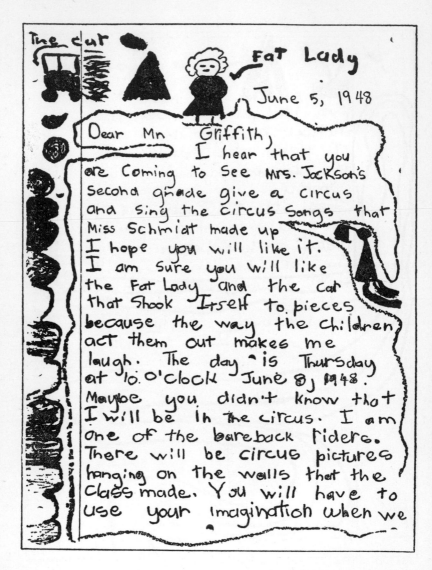

The car

Fat Lady

June 5, 1948

Dear Mr Griffith,
I hear that you are coming to see Mrs. Jackson's second grade give a circus and sing the circus songs that Miss Schmidt made up I hope you will like it. I am sure you will like the Fat Lady and the car that shook itself to pieces because the way the children act them out makes me laugh. The day is Thursday at 10 o'clock June 8, 1948. Maybe you didn't know that I will be in the circus. I am one of the bareback riders. There will be circus pictures hanging on the walls that the class made. You will have to use your imagination when we

Second draft, showing child has made

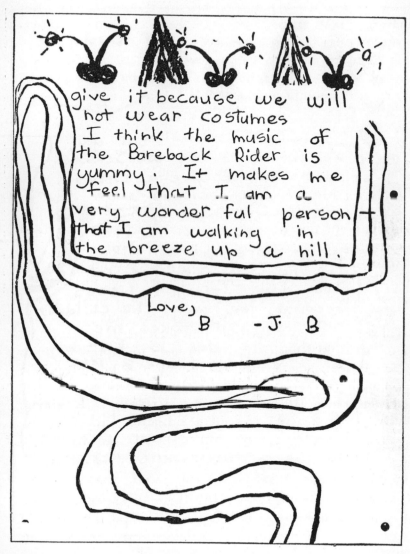

give it because we will
not wear costumes
I think the music of
the Bareback Rider is
yummy. It makes me
feel that I am a
very wonderful person—
that I am walking in
the breeze up a hill.

Love,
B -J· B

necessary corrections and "decorated" his copy.

23

for proper names and the beginnings of sentences. This is by no means their first exposure to these items of mechanics. Over and over again, as the teacher has been writing on the black-board, she has indicated the need for such marks of punctuation. Toward the end of the year children in one first grade became interested in taking turns writing on the blackboard the special appointments for the day. Here is an example:

Tuesday, Apr. 15, 1950

Music	9:25
Outdoor Play	10:15
Science	2:00

This was but one of many instances in which capitals and punctuation marks were used in a meaningful setting.

In correcting first drafts the teacher works with each child individually. As they are reading the letter aloud together, she pauses to ask: "What goes here?"; "Why do we need a period after Feb.?"; or, "Where does the sentence stop?" The time devoted to this is governed by individual needs and abilities. With the child who has had to struggle to express his ideas clearly or for whom writing has been a laborious process the checking is got over quickly; but with one who is more mature and who writes with relative ease, the editing is done more slowly, so that the child can take the initiative.

VARIED OPPORTUNITIES FOR WRITING

We value highly those situations through which we can lead children to care enough about what they are composing to give it a personal flavor. We believe that if a child is to grow in power in written language, he must learn early to respect his individual way of saying things.

Because one third grade found their lockers so small that precious papers were getting crumpled and torn they welcomed the suggestion of making storage folders for their unfinished

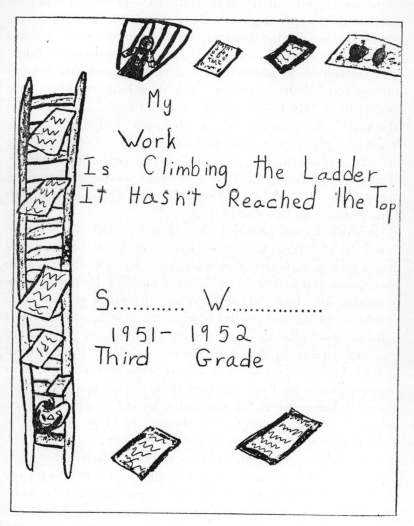

My
Work
Is Climbing the Ladder
It Hasn't Reached the Top

S............ W..............
1951- 1952
Third Grade

First draft of cover design for folder to contain unfinished work.

25

work. Since the folders would be kept on a shelf where visitors could easily spot them, it was necessary to indicate that they held material that was being worked on. Certainly we didn't want "company" to examine them with the notion that their contents were finished samples of writing. Here was a chance to dramatize the fun of "thinking up a title that fits, and that belongs only to you." "Of course," we suggested half-heartedly, "you could call it, 'My Folder of Unfinished Papers.' How do you like that?" By giving a title so obviously dull that everyone could disapprove of it we hoped to forestall any child's taking the easy, unimaginative way out. When our next question, "Has anyone a better idea?" brought no response, we tossed in, "Here's one — 'Work Under Way'; but," we added quickly, "that's ours. No one else may use it."

Suggestions came slowly at first, but we made no effort to hurry the children. Instead we commented on the fresh and fitting idea in each title they gave, such as: "I'm Loaded with Unfinished Work"; "Girl at Work — Do Not Disturb"; "Approaching the Finish Line." When invention seemed at a standstill, we showed on the blackboard how to arrange their titles for good placing. As we wrote each one, we pointed out how to capitalize it: In a title the first word and the last word and all the important words between begin with capitals. Our primary reason for lingering over these details was not to produce handsome covers. It was rather to stir up the children's pride so that they would exert themselves to do the kind of work that would give them earned satisfaction.

During the teaching interval most of the children had thought of titles; so all were given cheap newsprint on which to try out spacing, penmanship, and decoration. We went about the room, giving help or encouragement where it was needed. Sometimes we interrupted the class to share with them a pleasing arrangement or a design that carried out the idea conveyed by the title. This often led other children to think of different names or plans for their papers. Since the amount of writing involved was small, anyone could, if he wished, make several trial pages

Work Horses
Are
Half Way
Around
the
Track

1951-1952
Third Grade

Folder to preserve unfinished work.

27

Does Your Child whine when she or he gets up in the morning?

Come to the Institute

The New Sarah Lawrence President will speak to you Mothers and tell you all the problems you need to know.

A P.T.A. Institute offered opportunity for

Hurry and Run!

The Institute is about to BEGIN

Before  After

If anything is wrong — for instance not eating spinach — Come to the Institute and find out what to do about it.

P.L

writing advertisements that produced tangible results.

without growing fatigued. Such opportunities for experimentation are of great value because they strengthen a child's feeling of personal responsibility for the quality and the individual character of his output. He tastes the vitalizing pleasure of working, not for the teacher's approval, but for his own.

The making of the real folder came at a later period. Each child was given a large piece of colored paper, which brought forth pleased comments as it was placed on the desks. The use of this paper was deliberate — it was expensive and lovely and was something to live up to!

With their samples to help them, they tackled this final step soberly. Some used folded paper as a guide to keep their writing straight. In a few instances children asked permission to change the names of their folders. Many decided to use designs that were different from their samples. All these changes were approved after quick experiments had been made on scrap paper to make sure that the new ideas were satisfactory.

As soon as the covers were completed, they were placed on the bulletin board where they remained for a day before they were put into actual use. No discussion was given over to their appraisal, but the appreciative scrutiny that they received from their makers revealed how much the youngsters cared about what they had done.

Children thoroughly enjoy writing all kinds of advertisements and posters to publicize coming events. It is fun to invent slogans and write copy that will bring buyers to a cookie sale or Mother to a book talk. Here, as in the making of titles for work folders, the emphasis is on thinking, and there is a generous amount of oral exchange. A slogan is considered good if it is effective and original. It must catch attention and direct it to the copy, which carries the essential information. The writing, when it is finally done, is so limited in quantity that it is possible to exact a high standard of appearance and correctness. Illustration, especially if it reinforces the idea of the poster or the ad, is always encouraged, for it is one more way in which a child may put his individual stamp upon his product. We have found that when children care about what they are doing, they work far harder than any teacher would have the heart to require.

Because the sending of letters and notes provides an easy opportunity to give meaning and purpose to practical writing experiences, this type of communication is often used too freely. In fact, through having to write too many letters, children frequently acquire more distaste for the activity than skill in doing it. So we have used these other means to care for some of the invitations and announcements, and have reserved letter-writing for the special occasions when the warmth of their feeling helps to carry children through the sustained and usually arduous task of composing a good letter.

ORAL LANGUAGE IS BASIC TO WRITING

Although the foregoing experiences play an important part in the initiation of written expression, they constitute but one phase of the approach to writing. From the first day in school the program provides children with the opportunity and time for them to express their ideas orally. It is through the patient handling of this form of self-expression that we help them grow in the power to state their thoughts with honesty and clarity. *Abundant experience in oral expression is more important in the development of ability to write than the actual writing itself.* Through discussing plans, telling stories and experiences, and simply chatting with each other, children exchange ideas freely and develop the ease necessary to fluent writing. At first some participate very little, but they enjoy listening to others, and eventually they make contributions of their own.

There are some subjects that entice all children to take part in group discussions. Experiences during thounderstorms or being in parades, stories about pets, accounts of "the time I had the measles," or "when I went to the circus," reports of dreams — these and many more may start the ball rolling. Topics of this kind are popular when small groups are working and talking together informally. Often we join them and take part in the casual visiting. Such conversations inevitably draw other children to the scene, and in this atmosphere many an inhibited child talks for the first time in an audience situation.

FIRST REPORTS

Besides encouraging the offhand exchange of ideas, we occasionally inaugurate a class study that is purposefully designed to stimulate inquiry and discussion. This enterprise is an oral one and is fitted to the capacities of young children, but it follows the pattern that is used to guide the preparation for written reporting in later years. First-graders, too, explore a subject in great detail, using such source material as fits their abilities; they work with it long enough to accumulate a supply of facts and to clarify their understandings about them; and they prepare an end product that calls for expression in their own language. Although this book concerns itself primarily with written English, we feel that the oral prelude to the later written report has a place here.

It is essential to start with a congenial subject —some project that will kindle interest quickly and hold it for a considerable length of time. Live things always have an immediate appeal. Through the care and observation of some kind of animal — rabbits, polliwogs, a baby hamster — children learn exciting new facts and taste the satisfaction that comes from realizing that some living thing is dependent upon them. Having something alive in a classroom, besides a group of youngsters, takes a bit of doing and is not without its problems for the teacher, but it can yield dividends of far-reaching value.

One of our most rewarding ventures was the raising of some baby chickens. The children were so eager for this opportunity that they sat through several sessions of earnest consultation with the science teacher while they planned the right home and food for their guests-to-be. The talk was animated and full of curiosity. These children knew nothing about little chickens except that they were "cute and cuddly," and they had much to learn before they could take over the responsibility for their care. Questions spilled out almost faster than they could be listed on the blackboard, and many meetings with enthusiastic discussion were required to answer them all.

Please get us
25 lbs. of baby chick mash.
Mrs. Jackson's room
210

A genuine need for writing is illustrated by this order written in first grade.

At last the day came when a roomy cage was set up at just the right height for viewing and handling; and with much ceremony the children added clean newspaper and food and water and gravel to make it a comfortable and healthful place for chickens to live. The next few minutes were tense with expectancy. Then the door opened and a lusty peeping announced that the chickens had arrived.

Each child served many turns as caretaker, and the responsibility was always carried out with dependability and pride.

Dear Miss Greve,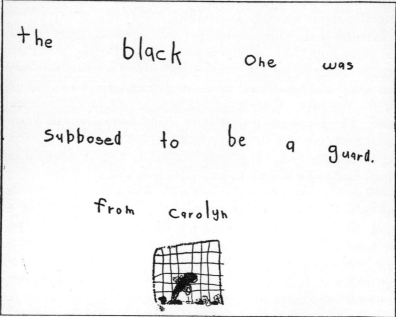

Thank you for taking our chickies home. One of the black chickens was up on the rock and the others were sleeping. Probably the black one was supposed to be a guard.

from Carolyn

A writing experience that came about in connection with the chicken study.

Every morning the appointed children were on hand early, often before the teacher had arrived, and they set to work at once to clean the cage, remove the babies from the warm box where they had spent the cool spring night, and watch with beaming faces while their little black and yellow charges chirped and ate busily. Always in the before-school time there was a gallery of fascinated observers. Older brothers and sisters, even teachers and mothers, stopped by for a look at the chickens, and on those occasions the first-graders were the experts who answered their questions with surprising accuracy and with the confident air of authority.

During class time there was abundant opportunity to talk, to watch, to question, and most important of all — to enjoy. This was such an absorbing interest that there was no need to hunt up things to talk about. It was a stirring and releasing experience that lasted long enough and was sufficiently dramatic to strike below the surface and affect each child so that he cared mightily about what he was learning.

Eventually the chickens became too big for the cage and so our janitor offered to add them to his flock. Parting with their pets was not easy for the young guardians. To help them over this emotional hurdle we proposed giving a chicken program for the mothers. Again the room was full of bustling excitement. There was much work to be done: decorating the room, making a frieze, drawing large pictures to illustrate facts, writing invitations to mothers, and finally, planning a program in which each child would play a significant role.

On the day of the program the room was lined with pictures and by ten o'clock most of the mothers were sitting in a large semicircle on the small first-grade chairs. The children sat on the floor in front so that they could stand easily and face the audience when their turns came. Anne made the speech of welcome and introduced the guests of honor — the chickens, of course. Shy little Ruthie was the announcer. She sat off to one side with the questions, which were written on big cards.

Her voice trembled as she read the first one: "Billy, how do

59453.

baby chicks get born?" But by the time Billy had explained
the hatching process she had gained enough composure to go
on. "Penny, why are they so fluffy when they are little?"
"Jonathan, when they get a drink why do they stretch their
necks when they swallow it?" "Jerry, how do we take care of
chickens at night?" "Lloyd, how do chickens chew their food?"
"David, why do they have little bumps on the sides of their
heads?" And so it went until every child had spoken. The
mothers listened intently, as one by one, each child stood up and
gave an accurate answer to his question, usually in words quite
different from the ones he had used when we had practiced.

Such unmemorized answers are factual reports at the first-
grade level. They are the culmination of an undertaking that
involved the whole child, both his mind and heart; that added to
his growing store of knowledge; and that extended his language
power.

FIRST STORIES

Just as experiences in oral reporting provide the necessary
background for report writing, so do the telling and dictating
of original stories furnish the preliminary steps that eventually
lead into the more mature technique of story writing. Fortunately most little children are interested in this form of self-
expression, and with very little encouragement from us — by
merely allowing them time enough for storytelling before an
appreciative audience — their stories show gradual but very
definite improvement in invention, form, clarification of ideas,
content, and individual flavor.

In one second grade almost every day children signed their
names on the blackboard under the caption: WHO HAS A
MAKE-UP STORY? At the beginning of the year, day after
day, the same five children were the ones who wanted to tell
stories, although with no exception the whole class enjoyed
listening to them. As the weeks went by, new children volunteered and their stories were received with enthusiasm. The

approving remarks made by the class had a definite effect on the stories that followed, although often individual gains were almost imperceptible at the outset. The changes in Kathie's stories illustrate this very gradual growth, as well as the amount of mediocre material that must be accepted.

Early in the fall, when she was in the second grade, Kathie told "The Family of Frogs," which the teacher unobtrusively took down in shorthand. In this she portrayed conflict with adults — an idea that runs through all of her stories and that was true in her own daily living. Although there is no evident story pattern, it was probably somewhat connected in her thinking but it moved so rapidly through her mind that she told only the high spots. The story reveals her vivid imagination and a suggestion of the moving picture she visualized as she told it. The sentences she used are the immature run-on type.

The Family of Frogs

Once there was a father frog and he was a big father frog and he had a great big family and he went for a swim. Mother went downtown to buy some groceries and the children were out playing and the baby was inside in his cradle. There was an alligator under the cradle and he jumped out. Baby started to cry. The mother came home and she came in and slid down on the floor. There was this pipe that led right out to the water and she slid right down it. But the baby didn't stop crying and one of the children came in. He tried to push the alligator out through the pipe, but the alligator was too fat and he decided that he needed a glass of milk. So he gave the alligator some milk and then he tried to push him out, but he got much fatter. The alligator's head was just peeping out of the hole. The mother came in through the hole and the alligator's mouth was open and she slid right down his throat. Down in his stomach there was this little house. She opened the door and she looked in. And she saw three ghosts, but the ghosts were friendly and they would not hurt her for the world of alligator's stomach. So they lived happily ever after.

In "The Naughty Little Duck," told less than two weeks later, she has limited her idea and developed it more logically. This time she was able to catch in words more of what was going on in her mind. The invention all centers about the duck who didn't want his face washed and she piled up incidents to effect this end.

The Naughty Little Duck

Once there was a little duck. The little duck was an awful funny little duck. One day the little duck went out to visit his grandma. His grandmother asked him if he wanted some ice cream. The little duck said, "Yes." And he went down to the ice-cream store and bought some ice cream. He smeared it all over his face and didn't like to have his face washed so when he got home the grandmother wanted to wash his face. He started to run all through the house and he slid on a rug. It happened to be that they had a vase that stood on the floor, and he slid right on top of the vase and it had some lovely roses in it. He landed on top of it and the water spilled all over the nice rug and the grandmother gave him a shellacking for being such a naughty boy. Then she took him up to the bathroom and she tried to wash his face, but every time she tried to get the wash cloth on he put his head down. He slipped and saw stars so he couldn't feel it and the grandmother put him in the bathtub and she washed his face. When he came out of being knocked out, he ran downstairs and he grabbed his scooter and he scooted home and I think that ever since then he never would buy an ice-cream cone. And he lived happily ever after.

A month later she related "The Family of Pumpkins," which shows remarkable growth in her ability to construct a well-knit story that works to a most interesting and personal conclusion.

The Family of Pumpkins

Once there lived a very old pumpkin. She had quite a lot of babies. They were very nice. They weren't naughty. One of her pumpkins was pretty. She was the nicest and kindest of all, but the others were jealous, and so she was treated very poor. None of her friends were jealous so she had quite a lot of friends. But her mother didn't think that she should do all the hard work, especially cleaning up the house. So she had the best fun.

"Of all the dirty tricks," said one of her sisters. "We have to do all the hard work while she goes out and plays with all her friends. She has too many friends."

The mother pumpkin said, "She has more manners than you. Until you learn how to behave you'll have to help me."

And so all the children tried to do good work. And pretty soon they had all the best of friends, too. And so they had to leave the mother pumpkin home to do all the hard work.

The last story, "The Fat Old Woman," was given just two months after the first one. Whereas the pattern is not so clear in her mind as the one before, her power to picture things vividly makes it more alive. The run-on sentence has almost disappeared, and has been replaced by more mature types, showing inversion, introductory clauses, and the use of verbals. There is also a pleasing rhythm effected by the balance of long and short sentences.

The Fat Old Woman

Once there lived an old woman. She was very fat, because she ate too much. Whenever anyone would invite her to their house she would say, "Have you got any turkey?" They would say, "No." She would go home. But before she went home she would buy a turkey. When she got home she would eat it. One day when she had come back from her shopping she found her dog gone. He was usually at home. She quickly dropped her turkey on the floor and opened the door and ran down the street. She saw her dog at the corner. Very quickly she went one way while the dog went the other way and they met. The fat old woman thought that she would take him home and she would eat all the turkey herself. She looked on the ground and she saw a run in her stocking. She thought she would go home and sew them, but when she went to get her dog, instead of her getting the dog, the dog got her and ate her up, but it took him a year to eat such a fat lady.

THE CONTRIBUTION OF DRAMATICS

The interaction between story invention and group dramatics merits a thorough analysis that can only be touched upon here.

The Good Witch and the Bad Witch

Scene 1

The good witch is trying to make some magic.

Scene 2

The prince came in and showed her some good magic.

Scene 3

The prince brings his father the king to the good witch's house.

Scene 4

The prince gets all excited about the bad witch.

Scene 5

The prince and his father and the good witch and her daughter capture the bad witch.

Scene 6

They shake hands and go home.

This copy was used by the announcer of a small group play. The description of the scenes served to make the plot clear to the audience and to remind the players of the forthcoming action.

40

We have found that stories and plays contribute immeasurably to each other. Both stir the imagination of children and help them to grow in confidence and power as they lose themselves in the excitement of living play characters. Our experience has shown, however, that each of these activities flourishes best when it is carried on without competition from the other.

By dramatics we do not mean the memorized-line type of play, for it rarely affords any opportunity for the individual to express his creative self. The plays that we do find invaluable are those created by the children themselves through the dramatization of book stories or tales of their own making. The dialogue for these impromptu plays follows a plot line, but the speeches are never written or "learned by heart" and usually vary considerably with each performance, just as the cast of characters may be adjusted, even at the last minute, to provide enough parts for all. Because there is no set script to be learned, the children are free to invent and to inject color without the awkwardness and the inhibitions that accompany the reciting of memorized speeches and with no congealing fear of forgetting lines. Moreover, these dramatic experiences are an outlet for many youngsters who through the disguise of play characters unconsciously reveal hidden facets of their personalities.

THE DICTATED STORY

Along with the many opportunities for oral expression the teacher should make it possible for the children to dictate stories and poetry. One way to initiate this dictating is to offer to write down a made-up story that has been of particular interest to the group. This invariably leads to a siege of dictating, with the children continuing their enthusiasm long after the teacher has been forced to call "time out" to rest her weary fingers. For a recorder who can type, these dictating experiences are not so fatiguing, and they enable a greater number of children to participate.

Little children enjoy dictating stories about pictures which

Program

1. The Circus Parade
2. The Barker
3. The Strong Man
4. The Talking Dog
5. The Singing Cat
6. The Fat Lady
7. The Peanut Vender
8. Clowns at Play
9. The Car that Shook Itself
10. To a Trained Seal
11. The Bareback Rider
12. The Dance of the Elephants

There will be no announcing between acts.

Preparing a program for his mother's use during a second-grade performance gives a child an honest reason for writing it in good form.

they have made. Sometimes a few pieces of Manila paper are folded into a booklet that is filled with pictures, care being taken to leave sufficient space for the teacher to write down the story that the pictures illustrate. We have found that in many instances children make the transition from this to another stage wherein they themselves write captions under the illustrations in these booklets, asking the teacher to spell needed words or phrases.

One of the essential accompaniments of the child's dictating experience is the reading aloud of his product. Naturally there is very little that has any outstanding quality. The teacher should take this for granted, realizing that out of great quantities of mediocre output only a little of artistic merit will emerge. In so far as she can, the teacher reads aloud everything that is dictated, but she takes pains to emphasize those bits of writing that, because of their originality and freshness of approach, will raise standards and prove inspirational to the others.

This reading should be planned carefully if it is to contribute to the child's recognition and appreciation of the creative expression of thought as well as to his growth in the ability to do it himself. Very few stories should be read at one time and they should be read well. It is important to choose periods when the children are relaxed and in a receptive mood. When they are too tired to sit quietly, they can get nothing from the reading. In such a negative atmosphere much that the teacher has been trying to build may be destroyed.

Three illustrations follow with the comments the class made after each had been read. These are stories told by beginning second-grade children.

The Little Piece of Chalk

Once there was a little piece of chalk. He thought he was walking on the sidewalk, but he was walking on the blackboard. One day he was wandering around the board and he came to a big, big house. It was a doll house. Something was hanging down from one window. It was a big piece of rope. He climbed on the big piece of rope and he ran up into the window. Then he saw the blackboard again. And he went on the blackboard and he drew a little girl holding a basket. The little girl walked in the bedroom with her mother. The mother couldn't see the piece of chalk and she wondered how that was drawn.

The mother said, "Well, I can't do anything about it."

So she went out in the kitchen and cooked the dinner. And the little girl went out to play with her friends. When dinner was ready the little girl came in and ate her dinner. After she ate her dinner she went to bed. The next morning she got up and went to school. And they lived happily ever after.

Tommy said, "I like the idea of making a story about a piece of chalk."

Peggy's comment was, "I think it was nice where the chalk thought he was walking on a sidewalk, but it was really the bottom of the blackboard."

Kathie said, "I liked it where the mother and girl were fooled because they didn't know who had been there."

Tommy with His New Teddy Bear

Once upon a time there was a little boy named Tommy. Tommy wanted a teddy bear. One day he went out to play. He looked in all the garbage cans. He didn't find any teddy bear. He came home and he asked his mother if they could go to New York. The mother said, "I'll think about it."

So they went to New York. They looked in every store. The mother said she was tired. Tommy said, "Come on, Mother, I want to find a brown teddy bear instead of black ones and white ones." So the mother said, "O.K., we'll walk to the next store."

There was the little brown teddy bear sitting in the window scratching his head. They went in the store. They came out again. Tommy ran all over the town, bumping into everyone with the teddy bear because he was so happy.

Harry thought, "It sounded just cute where Tommy saw 'the little brown teddy bear sitting in the window scratching his head.'"

Ruth liked the ending. She said, "Tommy sounded so happy, and it didn't say 'they lived happily ever after.'"

Frank said, "Grace made me see a picture of Tommy when he ran all over town bumping into everyone."

The Little New Pocket

Once there was a little pocket. This little pocket was sewed on a dress and he didn't like it. So this little pocket didn't know who wore this dress. So he planned to go away. And the little girl never went out of the house. All she did was look out the window at the big gray buildings. So all he saw was green and gray, because the dress was green and all he looked at was himself. Of course he had two eyes, a nose and a mouth and two legs and two arms, but he didn't have any teeth because he was a new pocket and the dress was new, too.

He planned to get away so he got off his hook that he was hanging on and tried to get out of the closet, but he couldn't get out of the closet. Finally he tried so much that he got out and looked for the scissor box, but he could not find it because it was moved to another place. He dragged the dress all around. Finally he came to the scissor box and just as he was reaching his hands out of the scissor box with the scissors the little girl came in. He lied down and tried to go to sleep, but he couldn't because he wanted to get away. He went snip, snip, snip, and finally he was loose and he wabbled around the room because he was a little pocket and he couldn't walk very straight. Finally he walked out of the door and he saw this man walking along the hall to this middle-sized box and it was very tall. He wondered what it was because he couldn't think very straight, but finally he knew. "It is an elevator," he said. And he saw a man walking out of another apartment.

The man went into the box and the door shut and it disappeared. So the pocket looked through the cracks and only saw the top and he dropped the handkerchief that the little girl had put in him one day.

He said, "I will be found out. They will see this handkerchief so I must take it."

He took it and he dropped the handkerchief through the bars of the elevator. It stuck in one of the ropes and the elevator got stuck coming up. The pocket squeezed through the bars and sailed down into the ventilator of the elevator. He rolled himself up in a long coil and squeezed through the net. He went sailing right on the man's head and he jumped off and thought he would get the hand-kerchief. He took the handkerchief out of where it was stuck. The man was in such a hurry to try and fix the elevator that he knocked the lever on. He went sailing up, but the pocket jumped up on the lever and pushed it back and stopped it. Then he pushed it the other way and it went sailing down and he went out of the door and out of another door and was outside.

He felt some drops. He thought it was raining, so he looked up and said, "Is that a cloud? No, it isn't." And there was the little girl crying. "My, my," said he, "I wonder why she is crying. Oh, I know — because I am lost. I must go right back."

So he went back and took a needle and thread and sewed himself onto the new dress, and he never took scissors and tried to cut him-self loose again.

The children loved this one and talked about it at length. They thought it was a different idea. The part about the pocket's seeing only green and gray interested them. They laughed when John said, "He didn't have any teeth because he was a new pocket and the dress was new, too." They enjoyed the ending because "it was not 'living happily ever after' and it ended quickly." And they relished the conversation when the pocket thought it was raining!

TRANSITION FROM STORY DICTATING TO WRITING

Eventually the time comes when children show the desire to do their own personal writing. In our experience this is almost always story writing. Usually, in the beginning stages, they dictate a paragraph at a time, copying each in turn until the story is completed. Sometimes they write down the first part of a story and dictate the end of it to the teacher. Finally, they reach the place where they are able to write a story alone, asking only for spelling help.

The transition from a child's dictating to the actual writing of his own stories is a matter of individual growth. We have found some who take over the writing of utilitarian material at least a year before they take over the independent writing of imaginative material. Probably this is because in utilitarian writing they can go back to sources if an idea is lost, whereas in imaginative writing thoughts follow one another so fast that they escape. There is no age limit when dictating becomes taboo. Teachers of older children who allow some opportunities for dictating are amazed at the impetus given to all kinds of story writing.

In contrast to their dictated stories children's first independent efforts are meager and disjointed. Although the story may be rich and complete in the child's imagination, his thoughts fly so fast that he catches only fragments of them in writing. The teacher, in her reading aloud to the group, must be able to "sell" these first independently written stories so that the writer feels satisfaction from having worked so hard. To do this, she studies his telegraphic style, talking it over with him, so that when she reads aloud she can fill in the gaps in order to make his story say what he wanted it to say.

A third-grade teacher used the following technique for beginning the independent writing of stories: She offered to help four who had already shown such an interest. Sitting at a large round table, the teacher wrote needed words on slips of paper just as fast as the children asked for them. This enabled them to turn out a finished piece of work before their energy was exhausted. Reading the stories aloud brought forth several requests by other members of the group for such an opportunity to write. In this way independent story writing began. Always the teacher made it a point to choose only a few for this writing group so that she might give help immediately. Therefore, the continuity of thinking was maintained, and the children had the satisfaction of getting their stories quickly into a permanent form.

THE TEACHER'S PART

Thus children come to know the release and delight of personal writing and to acquire pride in meeting the necessary

standards of practical writing. But it must be remembered that
this power develops best in a setting that is rich and meaningful
to children. To achieve such school living is a constant challenge to the teacher. Not only must she provide a program that
is neither sterile nor monotonous, but she must safeguard children against being bombarded by so many interests that they
are confused, and their energies dissipated. We have found
that we get our best results when there is a nice balance between
satisfying experiences and time for their assimilation. Clearly
realized in the mind of the teacher must be the goals that she
wishes to attain and the steps by which she wishes to attain them.
To be sure, all writing for children is not dictated by this
pattern — normal growth does not proceed in a straight line —
but there must be a sense of moving ahead. Finally, all this must
take place in an atmosphere that is warm and appreciative. The
quality and sincerity of child writing dwindles to nothing when
fear and self-consciousness set in. If children are fed a nourish-
ing diet of experiences, if their underlying need for growth
is being satisfied, and if they are free to write naturally and
joyously, they grow in writing power and they mature mentally
and emotionally as well.

The bond of society consists of reason and speech. — CICERO, De Officiis

3. *Practical Writing*

*J*NVITING one's parents to a star party, as did David in the following letter, is a serious responsibility. If adults are made to see the necessity for an eight-year-old's going to school after dark, the much wanted permission may be forthcoming. If the message is not clear and convincing in tone the whole plan may result in failure. The months of study that have enveloped the third grade in white-hot enthusiasm can have a fitting climax if it can be shared with parents in plain view of the night sky. Reporting knowledge in such a setting would add prestige to the young workers who so obviously seek grown-up importance. Hence the children worked carefully in writing, correcting, and copying these letters of invitation. Similar in purpose to David's but different in phrasing, each presented information essential to parental understanding of the bona fide nature of the evening session.

✓ Elementary School
Bronxville, N.Y.
March 26, 1952

Dear Mother and Father,
    There will be a Star ~~th~~
party on Wednesday,
April 2, 1952, ~~if~~ it is not
cloudy or is not raining.
~~If it is, ~~ ~~put put~~ it will
~~be on~~ the next evening
~~that is clear.~~ I have to
~~rest from 4:00 P.M. till 5:00 P.M.~~
~~We are going to Show~~
~~Slides. We will talk about~~
~~Planets and constellations.~~
~~The party will Start at~~
~~7:00 till 8:00.~~ seven o'clock.

        Love,

            D

First draft of David's letter to his parents inviting them to the star party his third grade was having. His carefully copied second draft was proudly taken home.

Table of Contents

A third-grade boy made this table of contents for his star notebook. His illustrations and captions for Mars are reproduced on page 55.

Letters were but a fractional part of a study that filled many weeks. For the reports that were to accompany the conducted tour of the constellations were the result of much seeing, working, talking, drawing, painting, listening, and planning. Reading, too, was a source of information: the teacher's oral reading of books too difficult for the children to read themselves; the reading of star charts and pictures, captions and labels. But firsthand experiences were the bedrock for these learnings. These children looked for planets and constellations in the evening sky; they charted in their notebooks what they had seen. They went to the planetarium to view moving models of the solar system, and to see a film-made procession of the stars showing a whole night's star cycle in a few minutes. They saw and touched specimens of meteorites; they clarified these detailed, concrete experiences through conversation and through making many illustrative renditions of their learnings. Star charts, clearly organized notebooks (pages 51, 53, 55), and slides would accompany their talks, which were planned to show their parent audience how much they had learned about Saturn, Venus, Orion, Aldebaran, and other ear-delighting members of the heavenly regions.

WRITING AND TALKING INTERACT

Because of the sheer labor of handwriting it has seemed to us more productive to make extended reporting for our third-graders an oral affair. For these children the rounded exposition of ideas needs, we believe, to be oral. Writing skills, for all their usefulness in plans, letters, captions, and explanations, are not elastic enough for the fluency demanded by these children's swift flow of thought. But segments of the whole cycle of communication inevitably are written; indeed, it appears in the star study, as in many another, that writing and talking complement each other. Recorded plans, titles, charts, and notebooks give permanence to the ephemeral spoken word. Illustrations are also part of the solid structure of ideas. They clarify under-

Story of Mercury

ME~~rcury~~ dent is the nearest *
planet to the Sun.
Mercury is the smallest
planet in ~~the Sun~~. our solar system. Mercury
is 3~~6~~ 36,000,000 miles from the Sun.
~~Mercury is farther away from~~
~~the Sun.~~ Mercury can go
around the Sun ✓faster than
the earth, On one side of
Mercury is winter and on the
other side of Mercury is summer.
Mercury always ~~turns the sun~~
keeps the same · side turned to
the sun.
← because it has a shorter
← way to go. ·

*Rough draft of a notebook page about Mercury. The correctly copied second draft
became a part of Mimi's star notebook.*

53

standing and provide a reliable nucleus for the oral reports. Further than this such visible materials to handle and explain contribute markedly to children's self-confidence by relating language both to manipulation and to the substance of ideas.

Throughout the star study this relation of talking to writing was reciprocal. Daily "star meetings" were held at which facts discovered and rediscovered were gloated over with the joy usually reserved for personal treasures. These informal chats about what the children were finding revealed a deep absorption in factual knowledge. Talking about the many fragments of information not only broadened the children's awareness of the range of man's astronomical knowledge but also led even these young observers to sense the necessity for grouping their many items of information. Plans for another meeting usually had to be recorded on the blackboard. Questions postponed for future reference were charted so as not to be forgotten. Books needed for special items were often listed. And as the idea took shape that an evening meeting with parents would be the happiest climax for the long study, many plans had to be jotted down: plans as to who would give which topic, and where each part of the program was to be held, since some of it inescapably had to be out-of-doors.

Writing made possible the more precise arrangements for the anticipated program. Writing made possible the creation of the notebooks that represented a serious organizing effort for these third-graders. The table of contents on page 51 suggests the orderliness that helped to make the copiously illustrated books an effective record. The first draft of Mary's "Story of Mercury" (page 53) shows the careful correction that she was willing to work out with her teacher and to use in the final copy for her notebook. John's full-page illustration of the planet Mars indicates the combining of pictorial representation with verbal explanation (page 55). This twofold clarification of ideas served the young astronomers many times in their dealing with the expansive subject matter of stars, moons, and planets.

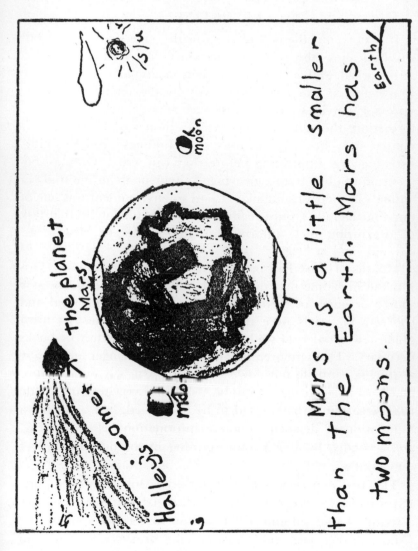

A page from a third-grade boy's star notebook.

55

ORAL REPORTING PRECEDES WRITTEN
REPORTING

It is not until the end of the fourth grade that most of our children show the maturity necessary for writing extensive, well-stocked, well-organized informational reports. Indeed, even fourth-graders can write well only as the climax of a long series of activities. They must first amass much concrete information; they must become deeply immersed in the subject matter; and, of course, they must share findings through talking, listening, and illustrating before they can write. Only as momentum resulted from a growing excitement about the study of animals in their various adaptations to environment was one of our fourth-grade groups ready for the difficult intellectual task of organizing their information and writing it clearly, accurately, and at length.

Months of work had preceded this stage of readiness. This was the first time that the fourth-graders had used books as a source of much of their information. Prior to this, real and concrete materials were the main sources of data. In third grade few could read well enough to use the variety of books necessary. Furthermore, the more serious danger of merely acquiring words to put down on paper, which is so often mistaken for true writing, had to be avoided. Even in fourth grade the menace of verbalism had to be forestalled, first by laying a foundation of detailed, concrete information before reading, and secondly, by giving some training in the difficult skill of note-taking.

The real experiences that introduced this study were prerequisite to the integrity of later individual writing. As part of a required study of animal adaptation to various climates, the children's own pets and animals living nearby were discussed with much warmth. Interest in these apparently random fact-finding meetings ran high before a beginning of organization was attempted. "What are all the different things it's important to know about animals?" was asked. With a bit of discussion and some re-ordering of suggestions a chart was made that included:

> Appearance
>
> Food
>
> Protection
>
> Enemies
>
> Where They Live
>
> Their Homes

These topics formed the nucleus of further sharing of findings about animals. More data were found in reading matter, in pictures, and from adults.

Getting facts from people who knew and from a number of excellent animal pictures was climaxed by a trip to the zoo. Here the prime questions were: "How does the animal protect himself?" "What kinds of food do they eat?" "How many babies do they have?" This building of factual background before turning to the printed page equipped the children with real meanings for the words they were to meet.

This acquaintance also provided the fourth-grade zoologists with enough contacts for them to begin to select their individual topics. Obviously each child could not report orally or in writing on all the animals of the study which ranged from the small animals near at hand — squirrels, chipmunks, and woodchucks — to those of the jungle and forest. Narrowing one's topic is as necessary in elementary school reporting as in the graduate school. "Take your time to choose the one you want to report on. Look at lots of books to be sure you can find good reading material before you decide. It's better to take time to choose than to change in midstream," they were counselled.

SEARCHING FOR MATERIAL

When four or five children had decided upon the animals they wanted to study, they were gathered together for some direct instruction in how to use reference books. Contents, indices, and the arrangements of encyclopedias were pointed out and their use demonstrated. A shelf full of the best books on animals was collected. Everyone was caught up in the excitement of the search. And, as so often happens in the quest for material pertinent to a given topic, individuals found as much for their neighbors as for themselves. "Say, you've got to get this book — you're going to need it when you get going on the elephant" was the kind of advice often overheard.

As the children began to find a number of references bearing on their chosen animal they, of course, wanted to preserve many of the details for their reports. Some started copying word for word what was in print. The time had come to lay a foundation for later note-taking. Each child was given a half dozen cards and was told to put down the name of any book especially good for his animal and the page or pages on which he found the material. "But I'll never remember exactly how many bushels of hay an elephant eats in a day," complained Henry. So facts that had to be precise, like sizes or speeds or weights, were agreed upon as the only kinds of notes to take. To copy the exact figures meant also the obligation of noting the name of the book and the page. This was enough of a writing chore to check the impulse to copy too many things verbatim. Sketches and diagrams were often suggested as better ways to get down an idea. It is unlikely that fourth- or fifth-graders can do other kinds of note-taking without descending to outright plagiarism.

How much to find out, how many more books to read were questioned one day when the searching and reading were going at full speed. "Look at the chart of things we thought were important to know about animals and see how much you're sure of," they were advised. (See chart, page 57.) "I know about the bear's appearance pretty well and about his enemies and how he protects himself," said Jon, in such a stock-taking. "I don't know all the places where bears live — there seem to be so many. I'll have to find more about that."

As the children found more of what they were looking for, their eagerness in the quest became more intense. Knowledge added to curiosity. The enthusiasm that springs from working in a company of eager fellow workers became truly electric. A few still feared that they would forget some choice bit of detail, but were willing to accept the adult promise that such matters could be taken care of later. Knowing that they could find the book and page again from their book card substantiated this assurance.

During this period of intensive reading two problems arose. As in almost any group of fourth-graders some children found reference reading discouragingly difficult. They needed help and they needed short periods for concentrated effort. One relatively simple device used in many study sessions was a notice on the blackboard SIGN HERE FOR HELP under which the children needing help wrote their names. The teacher was then able to get to these children in the order of their signatures, thus avoiding confusion and waste of time. The other problem was that of fatigue and what the poor readers (or immature readers) might do while waiting their turn for help. They were urged to make illustrations for their reports — pictures, an introductory announcement, a surprising statement of size or kind of protection, or a diagram showing, perhaps, claws and pads on a tiger's feet. The children kept in folders the pictorial material that they were getting ready for their oral reports.

ORGANIZING THE ORAL REPORTS

After two or three weeks some of the fastest workers declared that they were ready, that there was simply no more to be found about their particular animals. The whole class was assembled to consider how to make an interesting oral report. The children were told, of course, that they might start with any topic on their list of things to know about animals. (See chart, page 57.) "Begin with the topic you are most interested in yourself," they were advised. "For instance, if you are reporting on the porcupine you might want to begin with his unusual way of protecting himself."

Because children learn much from each other and because first examples in such a situation are influential, it was found expedient to give really detailed help to those who were ready first to report. These first reporters were asked if they needed help on any special part of their report. Perhaps an item of fact had to be checked or a more accurate reference for some moot point decided upon. But the teacher's main job was that of organization. "What are you going to tell about first?" was followed by her jotting down on a card the topic to use as a beginning. A sample of the sequence worked out with one fourth-grader follows:

Walrus

I. Introduction

II. Life and Use
  1. Where he is found
  2. Appearance
  3. Food
  4. Protection
  5. Family
  6. Home
  7. Enemies
  8. Use to man

III. Pictures—own
             real
             book

With this in hand for a guide and with much illustrative material to show, the reporter was ready and confident of his audience's interest.

This individual planning with the teacher took less and less time. As some reports were given in well-ordered sequence, the children become aware of what made a good report. They came to their planning conferences so well-geared to the job that it took only a brief checking to give that sense of certainty for which most fourth-graders still look to adults. The careful preparation that each child had made, the sense of group enterprise that had come from the real experiences and from the avid search for materials and sharing of findings, set the stage for active listening. Preparing the group to hear each report was as carefully attended to as when the first-graders shared their information about chickens (Chapter 2). Discussion after each report indicated that genuine concern had developed for the success of each speaker as well as interest in his exciting subject matter. After the oral reports had been completed, a process that took quite a few days, a week's interlude was allowed for better perspective before beginning the anticipated job of writing the reports.

STARTING THE WRITTEN REPORTS

One of the most difficult things about informational writing, even for many grown-ups, is getting started. Recalling the reports recently given, we began directly with matters of fact.

"What do you remember about the animal you studied?"

"Oh, I remember how fast the sea lion catches fish," volunteered Ken.

"And I remember how big the elephant is. A full-grown elephant can grow to be fourteen feet tall, about as high as the ceiling in this room," added Sue.

"Ken knows about the way his animal gets his food," we pointed out. "So, Ken, please write FOOD at the top of this paper. Sue remembers about how big her animal is. That's his appearance. Sue, will you write APPEARANCE on this paper? Write everything you know about the heading you put on your paper. Take a clean sheet every time you start on a new topic. Use all the different topics we had on our charts (page 57), and make up others if you need to."

The children were elated at having six or eight pieces of paper to start with and the idea of writing each different thing they remembered about how the bear looked or how a lion protected himself seemed to break down the Herculean task into controllable parts. The caution to write nothing else on the Food paper but what you knew about food and to take a fresh paper for Babies if you wanted to tell about them seemed a little startling at first. This sudden bounty in the use of paper had many possibilities that are immediately apparent. Rough drafts always need space for correcting. Further, the evidence that one is covering many pages adds impetus to the process, for children often feel that lengthy writing is related to grown-up status. But the most important outcome is that of having material so arranged that all one's ideas about food, or habitat, or protection are grouped together logically. Reshuffling topics and pages to fit the organization the child eventually decides upon is then relatively easy.

In the writing of reports we are concerned with two things simultaneously: that of making the product factually true and that of keeping the writing as individual in style as are the persons concerned. Once the children have got off to a good start with their packs of paper, we interrupt occasionally to ask who is writing something that is not only true but would also be fun to hear. Free of the inhibitions of adult writers, our children are eager to read what they have written:

Kim, for example, was excited about the way he had pictured the strength and speed of the tiger:

A tiger eats any unfortunate victim that he can kill. This includes man who is the slowest animal and the most helpless even with his guns. Sheep, goats, and cattle also are food he dines on. Any cow that is lagging behind a herd is immediately pounced upon.

It is easy to see why Ralph was eager to read what he had written about the raccoon:

A raccoon's use to man is his skin and meat. I saw a raccoon once in a store. It was lovely. My uncle Tom cooked some raccoon meat and ate it. He said it was fair. He couldn't make up his mind whether it was good or bad.

This spilling over of enthusiasm contributes markedly to the enjoyment of the difficult job. It adds the elusive element of group momentum. And further it demonstrates the fact that it is one's personal reaction that adds flavor and color to a recital of facts. Accuracy and the strength of one's writing are of a piece.

MAINTAINING INTEREST IN WRITING

Since in spite of enthusiasm, writing is a fatiguing occupation, we have found it wise to make these periods short. Once the children have got the feel of the thing, once they have caught on to the idea that they can begin with any topic, with whatever interests them most, the teacher plans immediately to forestall weariness. With the fourth-grade group here described, whose threshold of fatigue was reasonably high, we let the writing go on for about fifteen minutes. "Finish the idea you're writing," we then told them, "but don't start any new ones now." "Oh, no!" they objected, almost with one voice. "We can't stop yet!"

To stop when vigor is high is a productive technique. There remains the feeling that one must get back to the work tomorrow, that one is full of ideas. No better beginning for the next day's work could be conjured up. Sheets were clipped together and put into the children's folders. Next day a few minutes of telling what choice bits some were starting with — what Sue was planning to add about the porcupine's sharp quills or what Jack was going to tell about the tiger's babies — and everyone was off to write with fervor equal to that of the day before.

ORGANIZING THE WRITTEN REPORTS

After three or four periods it became obvious that the children were almost "written out," that most of them were coming to the end of either their knowledge or their energies. At this point we again gathered the class together to consider a further

step. Facts had been recorded accurately and in such a way
as to be interesting to the children. But since these reports
were to go home for parents, something else was needed. "What
would you have to do for a reader who picks up your report
cold in order to catch his interest?" we asked. It was clear almost at once that something which makes you take notice
immediately must precede the statements of fact about appearance, or enemies, or any other topic. Some children thought
that what they themselves felt about their animal was likely
to prepare the reader for what was to come. As is often the case
in adult writing, our children wrote their beginnings after they
had written the body of their reports. Here are some samples
of the beginnings with which the children planned to introduce
their reports:

There are too many kinds of wolves to suit me. I wouldn't like to
meet a mad wolf or a bad wolf but all wolves are bad I'm afraid.

The giraffe has a neck like a totem pole. His long neck might
seem funny to us but it comes in very handy to him.

The old grouch with the whiskers and the two ivory tusks is the
walrus.

CORRECTING AND COPYING THE REPORTS

The only tasks now left before the finished reports could be
taken home were those of editing and copying. Reading aloud
together, correcting spelling and punctuation as they went
along, pupil and teacher cleaned up the first draft. In some instances the children discovered shortages of fact or ideas hazily
expressed. Dictating the revision to the teacher eased the labor
of making corrections. The importance of a carefully planned
conference gave to the work the dignity required for this last
important step of editing, which must not be allowed to take
on the atmosphere either of anticlimax or of negativism. When
all the necessary patching of expression or mechanics was complete, the reports were ready for copying.

Putting the finished copy and illustrations into a folder to take home was an easy and pleasurable task. The contrast between the finished copy and the corrected rough draft, with its erasures, crossed-out words, arrows and stars for insertions, was gratifying. The fourth-grade reporters were proud of their well-oganized, accurate results and infinitely pleased with themselves and their new accomplishments. The report that follows is an average one resulting from this study.

INFORMATIONAL REPORT

Here Comes the Woodchuck — Big, Fat, and Handsome

Out in the open spaces where there are rocks the woodchuck builds his home so that the bears and the dogs can't get him. You could find the look-out tower. It is made from the dirt that he has dug out while he was building his home.

A woodchuck's home is a burrow which he digs under stonewalls. He spends most of his time eating vegetables like carrots, corn, lettuce and all young vegetables. Farmers do not like it because woodchucks raid their gardens.

If you go over to the woodchuck's home you'd find four to nine babies so that's why every time the farmers shoot one they can't get rid of them because there are so many more than they can shoot.

Their protection is their home mostly. They use their tower to see if any enemies are coming and when they do come, the woodchuck goes in head first and if the enemy comes while their babies are playing outside the woodchuck whistles for them to come in the hole. When the dogs try to get in the hole, the woodchuck just goes out the back door and watches the dog digging away. When the woodchuck is surrounded he'll snap his teeth and claw like a cat.

EXTENDED REPORTING IN LATER GRADES

As experience accumulates, the responsibility for saying clearly what one wishes to report continues to be personally felt. Control of factual data, greater reading power, and longer attention span all contribute to the extension of reporting ability. Other factors also influence this greater strength. Intimate and genuine association with a wealth of literature makes it inevitable that children should absorb something of the familiar patterns of folklore and fairy tale, something of form and idiom, something of the rhythm and cadence of our language.

The sheer bulk of prose consumed by the average voracious reader of eight to twelve may partly account for the tendency toward more voluminous expression. It also seems true that the respect for honesty in practical writing and the opportunity for sincerity in personal expression make children much more sensitive to color, or ruggedness, or fragile delicacy, or exact phrasing in what they hear. One group of sixth-grade children upon hearing *Moti Guj, Mutineer* picked out spontaneously many of those elements that make Kipling's style the inimitable delight it is.

"Oh, read that again, please — where he called him 'warty toad of a dried mud puddle,'" asked Alice.

"And read all those other things Deesa called him," asked another. "They're swell."

"That part, too," remarked Jerry, "where Moti Guj swung the baby up in the air in his trunk — that was awfully smart. Gosh, he certaintly *had* Chihun there."

"There's something alike in all Kipling's stories and yet every animal is different. He uses so many big words! If we try to use big words in a story just to use them — well, it just sounds queer, that's all."

And again out of thousands of instances that might be recalled:

> "A prompt decisive man, no breath
> Our father wasted: 'Boys, a path! . . .'"

when heard by the same group one snowy winter day brought from mischievous Albert, "Oh, boy, I know what kind of man he was! Just two lines to say all that." Whittier's economy of description was not lost upon children who had themselves felt the compulsion to make their characters real. Moreover, this heightened awareness made them infinitely more responsive to those few elements the teacher chose to bring to their attention.

So interwoven are these lines of growth in extended reading, in personal and practical writing, in genuine literary appreciation — so tied up are they with the whole business of growing up — that it is truly impossible to separate cause from effect, or ends from means. Reading, hearing, telling, listening, and writing become mutually significant. A many-faceted sensitivity emerges through an alchemy we little comprehend. But though we do not understand the process, at least we know that two of the indispensable elements of this genuine integration are time to assimilate and opportunity to react honestly.

An example of this more facile and extensive expression is to be found in a report written by a child of eleven. Though this is an instance of practical writing, of reporting information to a larger class venture, we note the individual flavor of "many a river has its beginning," "the salmon also have their beginning," or "something like instinct tells them to go back." Carolyn was a spirited child and her interest in the live creature was reflected in the quality of her writing about the journeys and struggles of the live fish. Her description of the canning process is dull by comparison, though the facts are presented in a fashion not greatly inferior to the average adult-written textbook. Carolyn needed checking only on the spelling of "uncertain" and "appearance."

Salmon

In Washington and Oregon on the tops of mountains, many a river has its beginning. These little streams rush madly along, fed by the melting snows of the glaciers. The salmon also have their beginning in that freezing cold climate. Their eggs are orange mixed with a little pink. When the baby salmon hatch they eat almost everything smaller than themselves. (By the way they are only about one-half inch long.) When they grow bigger they finally start downstream to seek their fortunes. When they reach the ocean they live there about three or four years. After this time, something like instinct tells them to go back to the streams where they were hatched. Millions of salmon start up the long, hard journey. Many of the salmon are caught or killed. The ones that escape continue their fight upstream, leaping falls and etc. When they reach their destination, the male scoops out a hollow in the gravel. Then the female lays her eggs and the male buries them. Then the two salmon float tail downstream and die an uncertain death.

The salmon that are caught are loaded into scows and taken to the cannery. Their heads and fins are cut off, and the eggs removed. The body is passed beneath circular knives. They are cut into the sizes of the cans they are to go into. Then a machine fills them in correctly. The cans pass on a belt to a weighing machine. Two girls in white uniforms refill any can underweight. Then the cans are lacquered because it gives the cans a nice appearance and also because when a ship is loaded with cans of salmon and is going south, it prevents condensation.

The people that are usually employed are either Chinese or Indians.

REFERENCES

Atwood and Thomas, *North America,* pp. 244-245.
Allen, *United States,* p. 253.
Pamphlet, *The Salmon.*

It seems strange to the logical mind that the cover in which a bit of informational writing appears should be of titanic importance. Yet to the child the delight of making a red back for his elephant book is at least of equal importance with the material itself. And rightly so. For the youngster the product is a total in which size and color and illustration are inseparable from content. Indeed, let any adult tell his neighbor he's writing a book and the amost invariable comment is, "Oh, I'd like so much to *see* it." Moreover, quite a few grown-up authors confess in unguarded moments that they see their book-to-be, printed, bound, standing in majesty upon the library shelf long before the first chapter is completed! As children grow up they take great pride in making by hand more interesting, often more complicated, types of books. In our experience no other activity gives more zest to the growing ability and interest in utilitarian expression.

OPPORTUNITIES FOR BRIEF PRACTICAL WRITING

Caution must be exercised against requiring too much writing even at nine or ten. Rather that a child in a whole year should write one report containing real substance than ten that become mere shadows. Of course, in most schools there is a continual need in upper grades for writing that affords practice in the mechanics of sentence formation, writing, and capitalization:

Keeping one's own reading list, month by month

Recording weather and temperature data

Recording feeding and growth of pets

Invitations and messages of all sorts, to people hard to see in person or too busy to be interrupted

Thank-you notes

Notices about assemblies, journeys, school bulletins, playground arrangements

Identification cards for various files

Spelling exercises, both the statistically derived lists and "our own" words; also dictation exercises

Recording absence and attendance daily for the principal and the nurse

It is highly important that children realize fully the significance of such records so obviously practical as those above, or else this sort of writing, too, can degenerate into a meaningless chore. It scarcely needs to be stated that doing these "useful" things well either may become a burden or may further establish that pride of workmanship that is in itself an energizing influence. Though a certain amount of practice in handling paper and pencils seems necessary to make it easy, the meaning of and attitude toward the writing done seem largely to determine how much practice there must be. Certainly it is less when situations are real and the reasons for accuracy are keenly felt. Then, too, increased maturity leads naturally to somewhat more lengthy expression in many children.

Fuses

If you will look closely at a blown out fuse you will see that a piece of metal was once attached from one side of the fuse to the other. When there is a short circuit in your house—by that I mean if the insulation should get worn ~~off~~ off two wires—not all the way off just scraped off in two places—and they touched together the electricity will go from one wire to the other one. Then it will go back to the fuse box and come to the thin piece of metal. It will try to go through the metal but the surge of the electricity behind will push until that metal gets hot and melts. This breaks the circuit and saves you from fire.

good fuse   This ~~is~~ a bad fuse

First draft of an article prepared for a book on electricity made by a fourth grade.
The corrections and additions were made as the child
read the article to his teacher.

Writing that is done in response to genuine needs is conducive to greater ease as well as to higher standards of both form and content. The occasional isolated practice on a few difficult items, plus, in intermediate grades, the use of writing in spelling practice, all contribute to greater facility of expression and likewise to better muscular control. Most assuredly, in addition to all this craft-writing, many children will be artists as well as artisans. At ten many will be writing stories for the sheer fun of the matter. The production of even very mediocre stories, if written spontaneously and joyfully, makes a valuable contribution to a child's fluency, to his control over the mechanical part of the act of putting ideas on paper, and to the eventual control to be gained from much experimentation with the highly complex tool of thoughtful writing.

CLEAR STRUCTURE TO MATCH CLEAR UNDERSTANDING

Though we do not tamper with a child's imaginative or personal creations, certainly in the realm of practical writing there is a need and a place for direct and thorough teaching. Much of the writing of this character is done to be read to the class, to be put into a book, to contribute to a group discussion of some larger subject, or at the more mature levels, *just to find out how!* It often seems wise to have a child, especially one who is weak in this field, read his material first to his teacher alone. If there are sentence errors the two may correct them together. Usually reading a passage aloud convinces a child that "it says too much," or "it doesn't sound finished." If he doesn't observe the weakness, the teacher points it out, gives him several examples of ways to repair the bad spot, and *sees that he does it.*

Frequently children come for help faster than a teacher can be of real service. Many children as they write feel a need for clarification of an idea but do not know how to achieve it. "I want to say that there are three ways of tanning leather," complained Ellen, "but one sounds so much like the other that I can't get them straight. It sounds like one talks about softening the hide and the other two are like tanning — you know, to make it wear. I can't make it clear."

Ellen was really asking for help to clarify her understanding of a process. Wise child! Indeed, without this clear perception, sentence structure is bound to suffer. After she talked it out and saw the point, writing it was not so mysterious.

But Ellen had already half-analyzed her own problem. Other children only sense a difficulty and feel inadequate and uncomfortable. There the case becomes one of leading the youngster to spot his trouble and then of helping him work out the muddle. This is indeed a slow process, but there can be no glib prescription handed out by the teacher to all who need help. She must consider not only the material the child is writing but also, most important of all, this particular child's maturity. She must talk over the concrete problem with him and guide him in straightening out his tangle. Going back to experiment or to reread sources to verify information and chatting about the matter may be necessary to heighten understanding. For it is understanding that is basic to adequate and controlled expression. If through conversation she assists him in clarifying his own ideas enough to write them, making construction fit his thought, then he will be permanently strengthened by the experience. Even though costly of time at the moment, in the long run such guidance is more economical and more effective because it makes for greater independence.

Of course the most potent help comes from the other members of the class with whom the report is to be shared. The degree to which it is clear and understandable, or adds to the larger study under way, or illustrates for a younger group, let us say, how bees organize their hive — to that degree the report is good. The criterion of clarity becomes the children's.

The teacher watches, naturally, for positive illustrations of clarity, good choice of language, or some accidental use of a superior technique. In class discussions she sees that the atmosphere is kept friendly and free of strain. Emphasis of comments should be upon how clearly the ideas were developed, how one thought naturally led to the next, how interesting a certain picture was made. A sportsmanlike attitude of seeing how suggested improvements would make the thought clearer in practical writing can be acquired by almost every child. If he rests secure in the knowledge that in general he is "coming along in fine shape," he can almost always accept suggestion for a needed change. This is a test of mature rapport, achieved only by many months of living together. Whether or not the rest of the group gets the point the child is trying to make in writing is the important thing — a test almost as tangible as seeing that a handmade boat really sails. This is not a matter of pleasing the teacher. She is usually too ready to interpret inadequate expressions and sometimes has to "temper the wind to the shorn lamb" if the child in question be personally insufficient. Following the reading and discussion, the writers often see changes they themselves want to make. After all, even in the professional world, a play doesn't really "click" until it is tried out on an audience. Up to that time the playwright simply cannot be sure.

As necessary as air for breathing is a rich store of knowledge before children begin to write. Perhaps days or even weeks of observing, analyzing, experimenting, talking, and reading preceded Jim's story of the cooling system in an automobile. It is necessary to know much to say little, if that little carries its point home. Certain it is that much of children's non-sentence writing, of repeated *ands,* and ambiguous construction is caused by their having to write before they have anything to say or by having to write purely fictitious or sterile exercises. If any adult doubts this, let him try offhand to write an animated and lucid exposition of "How to Build a Skyscraper" or "An Interesting Conversation Between Two Natives of Tierra del Fuego." No more absurd than dozens we were asked to do in early childhood! Moreover, a child needs time to assimilate an experience, be it experiment, trip, reading, or observation, before the ideas gained can become part of his own mechanism. In our experience writing about yesterday's trip to the museum has been sadly unsuccessful. Or yesterday's picnic, likewise! Not even our most glowing enthusiasm has provoked a flow of ideas when the reaction to the experience was yet too raw to be translated into written form. Again and again this has proved true. Time for experience to ripen is as important a phase of the ideas-into-writing cycle as the actual putting pen to paper. Reflecting, talking, thinking about what one has done become necessary precursors to that condition of clear perception that makes clear writing possible. Indeed, even many able children slip back into non-sentence or otherwise faulty construction when forced to write what has not yet been digested and absorbed. Furthermore, the apparent correlation between repeated *and*s and immature mentality adds weight to the belief that a genuine control of ideas is the main condition for adequate writing. * Content begets form!

ACHIEVING MORE MATURE ORGANIZATION

Not only is clear construction an outgrowth of thoroughly assimilated ideas; effectiveness of organization, that much-lauded characteristic of real intellectuality, is also closley related to thorough understanding. But sound organization of material depends, too, upon other vital factors. True, a rich background of ideas is important. So, too, is the degree to which these ideas have matured within the individual, a process that takes time and that, if hurried, can produce only a mushroom growth. To let the ideas one has touched lie fallow, to sort and re-sort them, to talk over what one has discovered or read or observed or thought are as necessary a prelude to logical arrangement as is the gathering of factual data. This casual talking over of experience, reporting the results of one's exploration, is a vitally important stage in developing disciplined expression. Here half-understood ideas, vague impressions, begin to take form through simple and informal talking about "what we found out" or "what we have done." New questions arise. Relative

---

* R. Salisbury, "Psychology of Composition," *English Journal* (May 1936).

values emerge. Some clarification takes place from this simple verbalization of ideas. And the fact that talking is so much faster and less strenuous than writing makes such conversational stock-taking an economical step toward the eventual refinement of expression. Thus do ideas become an integral part of the person concerned.

Another factor in a developing power of organization is the clearness of purpose for which the specific material is being gathered and presented. Even to seven-year-olds, preparing a simple program to show their mothers what they had been studying about Scandinavia offered a problem in organization and likewise set the general scheme of their presentation. Mothers would see first, upon entering the room, the large fireplace and bed set up in one corner.

"We'll have to explain in the beginning about the big things because that's the first thing they'll see. We can tell about the cupboards, the pewter, and the red panels afterward."

Another group of eight-year-olds, in planning a star party for the seven-year-olds, realized that many things they'd like to tell (often just because they're so proud to know them) wouldn't fit into a party, and certainly not into a party for younger children. Seven-year-olds, from the vantage point of being eight, need things made very easy and very clear! Incidentally, explaining anything to younger children obliges one to be very straightforward and direct, a discipline most valuable to writers of any age. Yes, selection and rejection of data for a specific purpose was beginning to be practiced by these children. Even at the university level, choosing relevant facts in terms of a specific problem continues to be an important type of intellectual exercise.

But of equal importance with a wealth of ideas, and a clearly seen purpose toward which these ideas must be organized, is the stage of maturity of the person concerned. To give significant help, awareness of the child's development of orderliness must be in the foreground. This again is a very complex matter, influenced by perhaps more unknowns than we have yet dreamed

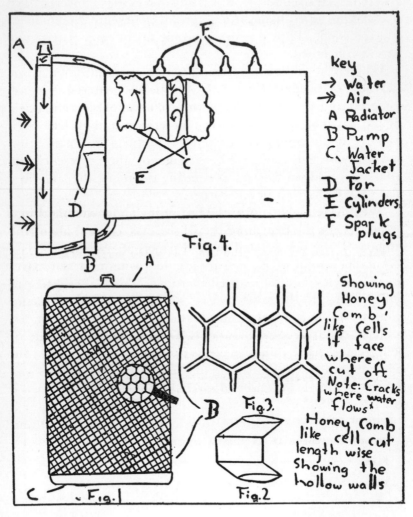

F

key
→ Water
⇒ Air
A Radiator
B Pump
C. Water Jacket
D For
E Cylinders.
F Spark plugs

Fig. 4.

Showing Honey Comb, like Cells if face where cut off
Note: Cracks where water flows

Honey Comb like cell cut length wise Showing the hollow walls

A

B

C   Fig. 1

Fig. 3.

Fig. 2.

From the book Automobiles *made for the school*

76

The Cooling System

The cooling system is used to cool the cylinders.
It is a very necessary device, for if it were missing
the terrific heat would stop the action of the cylinders.
To prevent this, the walls of the cylinders are made up
of hollow passages. These passages extend around the cylinders and form what is called the water jacket. (See
figure 4 C) You have probably seen on the front of a
car a honey comb-like thing which is called the radiator.
(See figure 1 B.) The radiator is made up of small,
hexagon-like cells. The walls of these cells are hollow.
(See figure 2 and figure 3.) When the garage man puts
water in the front of your car, the water enters atank
which is joined with the top of the radiator. After
reaching this tank, the water trickles down through the
radiator, or in other words it trickles through the
hollow walls of the hexagonal cells into another tank.
(See figure 1 C.) In the meantime air has been sucked
through the radiator crosswise; so at this stage the
water is quite cool. From the bottom tank the water is
pumped into the water jacket and cools the cylinders. To
recool the water it is pumped through a pipe into the
first tank, and the process is repeated from the beginning. Thus the water is constantly circulating.

library by a group of sixth-grade boys.

of. Differing with every individual, this mental power is a fascinating and a subtle one, growing with the growing individual; yet in no two persons does it show the same earmarks, even if they have been brought up in the same general environment, with apparently the same immediate purposes, and even with the same I.Q. To a degree, fortunately, a feeling for organization is a part of everyone. Moreover, it appears that the privilege of writing purposefully and sincerely makes a marked contribution to its natural development.

It is very interesting to observe some of the manifestations of a dawning sense of order. Even quite immature children often want to divide a report or a story into chapters, in an effort to satisfy their need for some sort of dividing line. The word "chapter" may seem a bit humorous to the staid adult, but it is by no means to be laughed at. Let the young writer divide his little offering on the fruit fly, let us say, into chapters if he wishes. In short order he sees that some of his items really belong in another chapter, one that will perhaps have yet to be written about how much damage the fly does the world over. This "bundling" of material, of putting like things together, is one of the first stages of logical and coherent writing.

As children mature it is easy to point out, usually following their own discovery of the matter, that within a chapter there is a sequence of ideas — smaller divisions within the larger one, the basis of paragraphing. That each different idea — each part of the chapter — stands out better if it is seen in a separate paragraph is about as far as it seems reasonable to go with elementary school children in this mooted matter of paragraph division. Certainly much of the trouble in paragraphing arises from forcing the use of a form before the need for it is understood. The groups under discussion had *experienced* the need for paragraph division for greater clarity. They did not learn it in isolated exercises.

Later on, children become aware of still another factor of organization, infinitely more involved than the grouping of like ideas and frequently conspicuous by its absence even in adult writing. This is the active principle in sequential arrangement. Yet the marshaling of functional material toward a real goal implies the beginning of a dynamic organization.

A group of fifth-graders, for instance, planned to explain the running of an automobile to another group similarly interested. Cogwheels, diagrams, batteries were at hand. Jack told how gas is exploded in the cylinders. Harry expounded upon the gearshift. Peter told how the battery, coil, and generator did their work. After the event was over, the children were talking about it with their teacher. Jim pointed out:

"I wouldn't have understood that. You know, we told how each part of the car works, but nobody ever told how they all went together."

The teacher's opportunity was at hand to point out that in many kinds of explanation it is necessary to "tie it together as you go along." They worked out, with little help, a plan showing how they could have done this with their automobile explanations, how they could have really traced power from gasoline to turning wheels.

True, an organization that lives, that is propellent and galvanic, is difficult to achieve, even for adults. Yet here was being used the genesis of this mature mental faculty. The children in question had the experience before they could understand the necessity for vitalizing their organization. Having sensed the need they could see what to do about it in a setting that was concrete and genuine in purpose. These boys had worked from a wealth of content for a period of weeks, had organized their learning for a purpose real and significant to themselves, had analyzed their talks in terms of how clearly they had told the story. With further similar experience these boys will be well on the way toward the exercise of an intellectual function cultivated under artificial circumstances by only the highly gifted.

As we encourage with cherishing patience the slowly increasing power of organization in written expression, it becomes signally clear that whatever plan a child follows in a piece of writing must be his own. Help may be received, but only after its need is felt; otherwise it is superfluous. Following someone else's scheme of sequence is a purely external procedure of no help to the individual and perhaps of genuine damage. The writer does not *learn to organize*. What the writer learns, in this case, is to imitate some other person's mental processes, to juggle words, perhaps to be clever. At the impressionable age this may be even worse than imitating another's voice, posture, and gestures. As given in one dictionary, the meaning of the word *organize* is "to give life or being to; . . . to cause to unite or work together in orderly fashion; . . . ; to endow with life." * Hence one is not organizing thought when one is fitting data into another's scheme. Obviously one is filling in a formula, fitting together the parts of a puzzle, giving an orderly appearance to the finished product.

True, the fostering of an individual's organizing ability takes time, but the process, because it exercises innate faculties, precludes long sessions spent on made-up exercises.

After extended reading, study, talking-over, note-taking, and more talking-over, Elaine, in sixth grade, made the following plan for her report on wheat:

   I. Planting and growing winter wheat
  II. Where it grows best
 III. Its value to the country
 IV. How it is shipped and stored

The last item, that of storage and shipment, was the teacher's suggestion but easily accepted as part of the job when Elaine saw its significance. After having read her account to the class, and while still satisfied with its acceptance by the group, the writer herself noted that she might have discussed the value of wheat to the country last of all, because shipping really "came right along after growing," but value and costs were something quite different and would be a better ending. Thus do experience and guidance interact.

---

* *The Winston Dictionary*, College Edition, 1944, p. 684.

Winter Wheat

Winter wheat is usually planted in September with a drill. It grows several inches high and then droops. It does not die but simply rests for the winter. It begins to grow again in the spring. Its color changes from green to golden yellow. Fields of wheat look like golden sand with a patch of green grass here and there with the wind gently blowing the wheat back and forth.

In late June or July the wheat is harvested. The harvesting machines have a thresher machine combined with them. The thresher has a little wagon that is attached at the side to catch the wheat as it comes from the thresher. . . .

Only about one-sixth of this report can be reproduced here because of the lack of space. Maps and graphs added to Elaine's three typewritten pages caused serious bulges in the original folder.

ENGLISH ESSENTIALS

Even with the best conditions we know — vitality of purpose, richness of background, confidence in the group and the teacher, much satisfaction in knowing "how much better we can do than a year ago" — even when all these conditions exist, a few common danger signals in the mastery of technicalities should be watched for. Clarity of expression seems often to be endangered by *then*s, *when*s, *and*s, used incorrectly. A reasonable test might be that Susan reread her three sentences, omitting *then*. "Can you feel the 'then idea' better without saying it?" An example follows:

(Before)

Then the blossoms begin to come out. The plants are then two or three feet high. The blossom is first white, then shell pink, rose-pink, and red. Then the petals fall.

(After)

The plants are two or three feet high. The blossom is first white, later shell pink, rose-pink, and last red. Then the petals fall.

Another frequent pitfall is the lengthy but incomplete sentence. When, in the process of growing up, the more able children naturally begin to use complex and compound sentences, such errors occur. "The switch on the line which was usually open where slow freights had to be side-tracked to let express trains pass." Having Ruth reread her lines to see what happened to the switch made her see how "where" caused confusion. *Who, when, where, which,* and *then* might come to be viewed with caution by the children themselves.

At times it is economical to isolate special ills of writing, observe them closely in one or several class periods, and work on them directly. The ever-present nuisance of showing possession is sometimes abated by an exercise such as this:

Dictated Exercises

We played "Snatch-Club" with Mrs. Brown's class at noon today. We had two teams and so did they. Jack's team played first and Mary's second. Our opponents were quick and well organized. They wasted no time forgetting their numbers. We won one game and so did they.

> Jack's books
> a girl's coat
> their balls
> their bats

The difficulty illustrated had shown up in previous work and many were aware of it. The teacher must point up this necessity, clarify the matter as concretely as she can, and then provide simple practice exercises to work on. Language texts, of course, furnish some helpful ones that may be used productively in this fashion. Perhaps a week or two later the genuine writing needs of a group of ten-year-olds may require the same items. Many will remember. Others won't. (Indeed all through high school and college "others" won't. Even in adult writing mechanics need continued attention.)

The following notice written for a real assembly two weeks

after the exercise on possessives made use of the forms that had been isolated for practice:

Assembly Notice

All children will please take their regular seats for assembly on Wednesday, February 10th. Miss Wright's class will give a play from the story, "Jane's Father."

For these and other more difficult items of English form some isolated drill seems necessary for almost all children. Correct use of apostrophes, punctuation of conversation, spelling of *its* and *their,* for instance, need to be spotlighted even after being used many times in a child's meaningful writing. Comparatively little of such practice is needed, fortunately, when children from the first grade on have held high standards of practical writing, and items of form have been supplied or checked by the teacher as needed. That such skills can become more nearly habitual after much correct use in concrete situations seems self-evident. Most important of all, after the habit of writing with fluency and with a sense of security and satisfaction has been established, these technicalities can be assimilated the more readily into a growing fabric of purposeful written expression, either personal or utilitarian in nature.

No real barrier exists, of course, between practical writing and those personal expressions that have been termed "creative." Indeed *practical* writing is also *creative.* Rather, these are similar, yet different, phases of the same social institution of speech and communication, differing notes in the same scale of verbal artistry. And, in spite of the great specificity of learning, we note that in the long run some transfer really occurs from the techniques practiced in utilitarian writing to the joyous artistic outpouring done for its own sake! From the beginning the need for clarity has for each child set standards high but possible of attainment. Continued, this has become a discipline, strengthened often by approval of fine work, by encouragement of obvious improvement, and on rare occasions by negation. The reality and often the dramatic quality of this approach is perhaps the strongest factor in the "carry-over" of standards from the practical to the more subjective and more personal writing of stories and lyrical expressions. When almost all of a large group of sixth-grade boys and girls volunteer to rewrite or retype a story to satisfy their own standards, the identification of the individual and his job has been clearly felt. The children have made a real integration between two distinct, but related, functions of writing, between themselves and the fruits of their labor.

In art what we like is what teaches us.
— E. DIMNET, What We Live By

4. Personal Writing

MOST of us remember all too vividly the ordeal of "composition time." No matter how zealous we may have been in filling private notebooks, we approached the same sort of task at school with distaste, if not with dread; and the prim, anemic accounts we produced under assignment were a far cry from the entrancing adventures we made up for ourselves when our imaginations ran free. At school we wrote to please the teacher; at home we labored solely for the joy of using our creative power.

Those secret stories that many children write for their personal pleasure or for the delectation of a few special cronies are usually crude, extravagant, and childish, but invariably they have life. Moreover, because their creation is prompted by an inner urge rather than an external compulsion, it works marked changes in the thinking and feeling of the young writers. It stirs and stretches their imagination, it develops a sense of ease in handling language, and it encourages the desire to make words say what they want them to say. These are significant changes that we wish to foster. So in our classrooms we have tried to approach those conditions under which children write spontaneously for their own fun and satisfaction. The stories they write are read aloud for our mutual entertainment, and no direct attempts are made to correct or improve them. In other phases of written expression we have redoubled our efforts to fix necessary English forms and mechanics; but in story time we have centered our interest on getting more and more stories because we have found that when children write copiously and with interest they make surprising gains in language power.

HOW STORY WRITING IS INITIATED

But the question arises, "How is story writing begun in the first place? When a teacher is faced with a new class, how does she go about stirring into life this storytelling power?" Our way has been simple as well as happy and fruitful. It is based on the fact that making up stories is not only a natural impulse but it is also a very contagious one.

During the early days of a new term we use short periods — "rest periods" we sometimes call them — when we gather the group about us and share with them stories that other children have written. Apparently the occasion is one for enjoyment only, but actually we are laying the necessary groundwork for future story growth. We are establishing the habit of appreciative listening, and we are implanting in our children the desire to do stories of their own. With ten-year-olds, for example, we might introduce them to the Bear family and then read John's story about bathing the cat.

It was early afternoon on a winter Saturday and Mo was calling his cat. "Here, kitty, kitty. Come, kitty."

His cat appeared, its black fur stained with mud from the melting snow. Ulp! No cat could be that dirty.

"Oh, Mo," called Mrs. Bear, "you'll have to wash your cat next week," but when Mrs. Bear saw the cat she quickly changed her mind. "Er — well, on second thought, you'd better wash it now."

"Now, Mother?"

"Yes, now."

"Well, all right."

Five minutes later Mo had the tub filled with scalding water. "I guess the cat would rather have it hot than cold," he mumbled. Carefully he picked up the cat by its tail. A howl rent the air, but Mo still held on. Slowly he dipped the cat in the water after putting half a box of dishwashing soap in.

"Yeo-o-o-ow." The cat wriggled loose and fell struggling into the water. Covered with suds he jumped out, spilling suds all over the bathroom.

"Darn you," shouted Mo, throwing a drinking glass at the fleeing cat. Crash! The glass flew into the next room where unfortunately Mrs. Bear was entertaining the principal of Mo's school.

"Help!" Then the principal came out very red and with the glass wedged very firmly on his long nose. "Good-bye, Mrs. Bear, and I must say that I never saw such a ——"

The principal's sentence was cut short by the cat, who was still trying to escape from Mo. Mo tackled the cat, or he thought he did, but the cat climbed the principal. Mo missed him and hit the glass on the principal's nose.

A little while later when they had gotten untangled — wack — crash — bam! Poor Mo! And all that night Mo had to stand up in bed.

This episode is so full of action and vividly told details that children can picture it readily in their imaginations. Quite likely they will make under-their-breath remarks about Mo's stupidity or the "poor cat"; and some adventurous child is sure to laugh aloud at the predicament of the principal. We laugh, too, because it *is* a ridiculous sight. Besides, we always deliberately contrive to read some stories in which children are aggressively clever, and adults can be tolerantly laughed at; for such stories dissolve the fiber of resistance, and are convincing proof to our children that they dare to write freely without fear of our displeasure.

The impulsive reactions during the reading will be followed, no doubt, by more comments at the close of the story. If not, we may chuckle over how clearly we could see the whole thing happen, and then, for emphasis, reread the lively action of the bath or the escape, or the picture of the irate principal "with the glass wedged firmly on his long nose." The mood we are trying to induce is a relaxed, companionable one with sufficient leisure to visualize the story and savor it to its full. Positive remarks are encouraged. If someone ventures a negative one he is reminded that it is always easy to find mistakes, but it is more fun to watch for the things to enjoy.

Since nothing stifles creative effort so quickly as adverse criticism, whether voiced or merely felt, we allow only appreciative comments in the story-sharing time. The tendency to pick flaws is checked in this beginning period when the children are listening to stories from the teacher's stock pile. To this end a few poor ones are always read. At the first negative remark we stop to discuss why we expect only approving comments or none at all. Our point is that if anyone takes the time and effort to write a story for our pleasure, we cannot be so ungracious as to pick it to pieces; and the children, through airing their own experiences, reveal how faultfinding takes the heart out of any activity. The exclusion of negative criticism is an absolute *must* for any successful program of creative writing.

The short periods of feeding stories for enjoyment are continued until two things happen: the children begin to show signs that they are ready to write stories, and the pattern of kindly acceptance is so firmly set that even the most humble effort will escape condemnation.

This whole process of initiation is of great importance. We find that every fall, whether our group be a new or a familiar one, a third grade or a sixth, we go through these same steps. It is essentially a warming-up process; the group has to be drawn into the rapport necessary to happy, easy writing, and the individual's own love of writing must be tempted to the point of action. With some groups two or three weeks will suffice; for others the preparation moves more slowly through a month or more, and there are occasional groups that require a whole semester of inoculation before writing gets under way.

Finally, when the time seems ripe, we suggest to the children that they begin writing stories. Our invitation is intentionally casual, and the way to respond is made easy. We provide a time for those who wish to write, and allow the others to turn to some self-chosen quiet work. The non-writers may do such things as read or draw pictures of story incidents, drill on arithmetic or spelling, finish up some uncompleted task. No stigma is attached to not writing, but acclaim is given to those who make the venture. With the occasional ones who are eager to try but who lack ideas, we visit a little, hoping to make a suggestion that will set their pencils going. If after a short conference no story plans are forthcoming, we council them to wait until another day. If a child has no characters in mind, he is free, we say, to use any from stories we have been reading. Whereas we once thought of an incident as the necessary starting point of a story, we now realize that many young writers invent with ease and originality when they begin with characters and let them act out their experiences on paper.

Because many children are blocked by their concern for neatness and correctness we urge them to care about nothing but getting their stories down. We write on the blackboard any words they ask for.

Stories don't even have to have titles. Starting with a title is often a limiting or inhibiting experience. Creative writers need the freedom that allows thoughts to wander as they will. To help a child feel more daring we sometimes remark, "You can never be really sure how a story is going to turn out; so it's an adventure for you, too. If you want to name it, that can be the final touch before you share it with the class." Many children forego titles entirely. When they finish one story, they grab more paper and promptly lose themselves in creating another. At the peak of writing excitement, ideas often come with a rush.

This whole procedure may sound careless, but we have found that it bears good results. Since our first concern is to free a child so that he can reveal his thinking and feeling through writing we must brush aside every hindrance that we can. True personal writing wells up from the subconscious, and unless those items which require conscious effort are minimized they can easily bar the way.

SHARING OF FIRST STORIES

When the first stories are finished it is a red-letter day, and a glad sense of achievement pervades the sharing time. As teachers we try to let no shadow darken this joy. For the halting or the fearful we read their efforts, having, of course, gone over them with the authors beforehand to make sure we can present them well. The more able or secure children usually choose to read their own.

During the reading period we give ourselves wholeheartedly to even the simplest story, listening as naturally and eagerly as we should like them to listen to us. Our eyes do not slide about to see who is wriggling; our mind does not concern itself with other matters. We give ourselves completely to the story, letting it hold us in its spell. By some curious form of osmosis this spirit of attentive listening spreads throughout the group. It is courteous listening, but more than that, it is creative listening, which works magically upon the children to release their native gifts and to build up their confidence. Even sophisticated adults are exhilarated and prodded by the *feel* of a responsive audience, and children, who are extremely sensitive to emotional climates, react more strongly still.

No early story is passed by without some sort of favorable notice. If no child volunteers an appreciative comment, we make sure to do so. In the most meager effort something can be found to enjoy: a hint of lively action or picture-making detail, a touch of invention, a curious name, or a glimmer of humor. Later in the year comments are often bypassed, but in the beginning they are important because they point up the elements that make all stories entertaining and alive. Moreover, they help to make the first storytelling experiences happy ones so that even a hesitant child will want to try again.

WHAT CHILDREN WRITE ABOUT

What do children write about when they write just for fun? Why, about themselves, of course! To be sure, they are not aware that this is what they are doing. They think they are making up adventures of an imaginary hero or a mischievous bear. But in reality, when they become absorbed in telling about Uncle Rufftuff or the Bossy King, it is their own experiences — their own thinking and feeling — that they unconsciously reveal.

Strangely enough, when a child begins to write because it's fun, he does not choose the topics we used to dole out as the easy ones based on immediate experience: A Summer Adventure, My Dog, My Trip to the Farm. He rarely writes openly about himself or about happenings that are recent and therefore fresh in his mind. The reason is plain. If he writes about himself he cannot write well about anything that has not yet become a part of that self. Only when experiences have had time to sink into deeper levels of a child's consciousness and there be intermingled with the residue of other experiences and other meanings, do they become the stuff out of which his imaginings and interpretations are fashioned.

As he grows in writing experience he draws more and more from this reservoir of emotions and ideas, and through the alchemy of his imagination he transmutes them into stories and poems uniquely his own. The world portrayed in this writing is essentially a child's intuitive creation — a most satisfactory world, indeed, in which the familiar and the wished-for are happily blended. He rarely peoples it with everyday characters, perhaps because he does not choose to be limited to pedestrian reality. So animals or half-fairy-tale beings take on the attributes of humans, while at the same time they accomplish with ease what is ordinarily impossible. It is an upside-down world as well, in which the child, not the adult, is the person of importance. By means of magic, shrewd intelligence, or merely a slingshot, he dominates each situation.

More than this concerning the substance of children's writing we are not ready to say. It is true that when they write without restraint, they write about themselves, but as yet we are not satisfied with our understanding of what those selves are really like. We do know that they are very different from adult selves in their desires, sense of values, and points of view; and also that they change markedly in the various stages of their growth. Realizing this we are slow to take exception to ideas that at first glance seem discourteous or crude. They may not appear so to a child, and we would only bewilder him with seeming injustice were we to reprove him. So we try not to curb his fun of writing by quibbling over differences inherent in our points of view.

On the contrary, we seek to open those channels through which natural child thought and language flow. Contagion is one of the most effective means we have yet discovered. When a few youngsters have grown excited about a group of lively characters or a new pattern of writing, their enthusiasm spreads throughout the group until most of the class gets caught up in the story-making activity. The fact that a familiar thread runs through their stories seems to add to the children's interest, and to free their creative power. Writing comes more abundantly and is of better than usual quality. Under such impetus some children produce the only spontaneous writing they ever do.

One fall a group of nine- and ten-year-olds came upon Sterling North's simple adventures of five little bears. The next day an original five-bear story appeared, and immediately the contagion began to spread. Every child wrote at least two or three stories about the bears and one boy wrote more than twenty-five. Although they used the same characters and frequently the same type of mischievous incident, their tales were remarkably varied, both in content and style. Curiously enough, too, of the large number of stories written that year the bear stories were outstandingly the best. Here is one of them; others appear elsewhere in the book.

A Bear Story

"Children," said Mother, "you are going to take lessons in language."

"How many do we have to take?" asked Nig.

"Four," said Mother, "Greek, Latin, German, French — now that I think of it you should have Spanish and, of course, English."

Mother had studied language and wanted the little bears to, but Father disagreed with her. He had gone away for a year, and Mother jumped at the chance.

"You shouldn't have to take them all at once, but you have a year and I won't make you go to school."

Just then they saw Father coming up the walk. "I am going to tell Father unless you promise that we won't have to take languages and you'll promise to take us to the movies ten times each month and let us go swimming every day this month," said Nig.

"All right. Don't tell him."

Father opened the door. "I forgot my suitcase," he said. "The boat doesn't sail for an hour."

The invention of characters is a difficult step for children, and newly created ones usually produce in their writing the formality and self-consciousness that one feels with strangers. But if children have characters at hand — old friends with whom they have laughed and teased and adventured — they find it relatively easy to use them as vehicles for their imaginings. When we remember the great story cycles, such as Robin Hood, King Arthur, and even our own Paul Bunyan, we realize that the community use of popular heroes has long been the story-teller's privilege and practice.

Furthermore, if these familiar characters are a compound of realism and fancy they make invention easier still. Although such beings may behave like humans they are not bound by ordinary limitations and standards. This sets a child's imagination free. His story people can wander at will between the real world and the unreal, they can combine the magical and the commonplace, and they can act in arrogant and startling ways that children dream of but dare not emulate.

For our own children the roguish bears — Eenie, Meenie, Meinie, Mo, and Nig — have long given lively impetus to story writing. From time to time we have suggested that some one devise a new set of characters, and an occasional child has done so. Dixie had her Otter Family — Big, Middle-Size, and Small. When the baby came she named it Tiny. John invented The Great Chimino, and Donald wrote many stories about Droopy, the Little Aeroplane. But by and large few newcomers have challenged the popularity of the bears. That does not mean, however, that there has been no invention of character, for in the guise of friends, enemies, and relations there have been many colorful additions to the original five until now the group of Bear characters makes up a sizable clan. There have been the baby — Daisy May, Uncle Upper Bumper, Eenie's boon companion — Roy Bear, Meinie's girl friend, and a host of cousins and playmates. If children are possessed of a set of characters as a nucleus they seem able to evolve new ones readily enough whenever the need arises. For their wonder-working power we have blessed and cherished the Bears. No other characters have inspired so many spontaneous, entertaining stories, nor released such an abundance of humor.

The tales about such imaginary, childlike creatures are unusual in their fresh originality. This fact shines out more clearly when they are contrasted with the realistic stories that children sometimes attempt. In concocting a horse or dog story a child commonly apes the situation, the vocabulary, and even the cadences of the animal fiction he reads. Almost never is there anything in his tale that bears the stamp of the author — no childish insight, no natural awkwardness of expression, no humor. A similar lack of inventiveness and personal flavor generally marks stories about everyday people. Ordinary characters rarely touch the wellsprings of imagination, but fall instead into dull, conventional molds. 'Tis the half fanciful characters that set invention working, and the disarming, familiar ones that reveal most clearly what a child actually thinks and feels.

It follows that because we permit each child to say what he wants to say in his own way, we, for our part, must accept graciously whatever he writes. Writing is a heart-warming delight when children are sure of an eager acceptance of their stories. Although many children like to write in an almost fierce privacy, they usually look for an audience as soon as they have finished. After all, stories are invented to be told to others. The joy of devising a story is only half realized until the tale is shared, and the delight of creation is reinforced by the pleasure of appreciation.

Younger children know of our interest in stories because of their previous happy experiences with dictating and telling them. It is quite natural, then, that they should bring their first stories to us. The word "bring" is worthy of note. We do not collect stories; we do not demand that they be handed in on a given date or as soon as finished; we do not even *ask* to read them; we wait until the children, quite of their own accord, bring them to us. Then we accept them as we would any other gift — with warm appreciation. Criticism is as inappropriate in this situation as it would be at Christmas time.

The teacher is definitely in the role of recipient. And it is a *story* that is offered, not an exercise in composition or punctuation or spelling. A *story* is offered — it would be absurd to talk of periods or paragraphs, of spelling or neat writing. Those matters are taken care of in practical writing. Here is a tale woven out of this child's unique experience, feeling, and imagination. To him the story is satisfactory and complete. We accept it eagerly, just as it is, without suggestion for change or improvement.

This is not always easy, for the desire to show him how to make his story better is a deep-rooted one. We may feel that it could be improved by developing this idea or cutting out that one, but we also know that if it is to be the *child's,* it must be

left in just the form which at the moment seems good to him.

Here is a story written by Peggy when she was barely nine. We are unable to reproduce the smudgy, wrinkled paper, but the story is otherwise exactly as she wrote it.

Grandmother's Skirt

Once there lives an old laddy with gray hair, dubble toes and a very sweet hart but she allways fell down becase her peticoat was allways hanging. She lived all alown way way on the tip top of a great big hill one of her hobies was baking pies blueberry chery and apple were her very best. The only one in all the world that she loved was her own grandbaby who hardly ever came to see her. Today however she was in her living room when a nock came at the door. She jumpd and ran to see who was coming, she opund the door and to her serprize no one was there she was all setled down again when another nock came. Again she went to the door and there she saw her grandbaby whose mother had got run over she had taken lots of monny so she could live with her grandmother and they bilt a new house and were very happy. After that the grandbaby allways held up her grandmothers peticoat and she never fell

Now it would be easy to criticize this. "What does baking pies have to do with the story? You haven't explained why there wasn't someone there the first time she heard a knock. Why not leave that part out? Whatever are 'dubble toes'? You need a lot of periods and capitals and your spelling is a disgrace."

Of course from the point of view of a nine-year-old, food is always a splendid thing to have in a story, "serprizes" never fail to interest, "dubble toes" sound fascinating, and periods and spelling don't affect a story anyway! So perhaps the very changes that, from an adult point of view, would strengthen the tale, would really spoil it entirely for a nine-year-old audience and would most surely have spoiled it for Peggy.

We read the story eagerly, ignoring the unconventional spelling and punctuation. We admired the amazing idea of "dubble toes" and pointed out that probably no one ever before had thought of writing a story about a hanging petticoat. We commended the way the story was rounded out, beginning with the petticoat and ending with it. Peggy beamed and volunteered that she had "a lot more ideas for stories even better than this." The story was read to the class, who added their approval.

Perhaps if we had criticized "Grandmother's Skirt" or any of the dozen mediocre tales that followed, Peggy might never have written this delightful story. For ease of reading we have corrected spelling and punctuation.

The House That Echoed

Once there was a sweet old lady who lived all alone with her parrot in a huge, big house with 143 rooms. She might have been a happy lady but she wasn't because whenever she said anything she heard an echo. There were echoes in every room. When she said, "Good morning, Polly," she heard high and whispery, "Good morning, Polly." (*The echo was always written very small.*)

When the parrot said, "Polly wants a cracker," the little old lady would hear, "Cracker, cracker, cracker," echoing all over the house.

She was determined to stop the echoes and to live happily ever after. She sent for some men to come out from the city to put hangings on all the walls of the 143 rooms. (*New hangings had just been put in our music room to deaden the reverberations there.*)

But when the men had gone she said, "Well, now *that's* fixed." And all through the house she heard, "Fixed, fixed, fixed."

"What shall I do?" cried the sweet old lady. "I know. I'll open the windows and doors and then the echoes will slip outdoors." So she opened and opened all the windows and all the doors in the 143 rooms.

"*Now* I won't be bothered any more," she said with a sigh, settling down.

"Any more, any more, any more," whispered the echoes.

"Oh, oh, oh," cried the little old lady and she ran out of doors into the woods. She walked and walked trying to think what to do next about the echoes when suddenly she heard an awful crying. She ran through the woods and found a whole lot of children, 439 children, all sitting in the woods, crying.

"Goodness gracious," said the little old lady. "What are you crying about?"

"We used to live in an orphan but it burned down," said a boy.

"Well, blow your noses and come home with me," said the little old lady.

So they did and all those children filled the house so full of noise because of pillow fights and not wanting to wash, especially the boys, and asking where things were, that there wasn't any room for echoes at all. And the old lady was happy. So were the children.

The following story is typical of the kind of thing we have learned to accept as cordially as we did *The House That Echoed*, overlooking the weak, confused plot, but calling attention to the spark of real insight — in this case, the quick characterization in the first four sentences.

In a bee castle there lived a cross old queen bee. She kept every bee over-busy. The king was kindhearted. He couldn't bear the queen himself. Soon he decided to get the "S" band. This was a band of stingers, stingers and selfish. The queen had many more ladies than the king had men. She forced the ladies to fight.

In two weeks, in our time, the queen got a rose with an invitation written on it. It said as follows: "You are invited to fight the King's 'S' band. Bee-bee." (The bee-bee meant answer soon.) The queen was expecting this and answered back, "Yes."

When the day came there was a carpet of bees' wings they lost during the fight. There was a bee called Octar. He was a "selfish." He was the king of the "selfish."

When the battle was over he was the only dead. Guess who won.

We read this story to the children with sufficient vigor to support the feeble plot. Nancy was happy that everyone liked her picture of the king and queen — and started another story. By accepting without criticism even this halting tale we kept the way open for her further writing.

Inevitably there is an occasional tale so utterly hopeless that one's heart sinks before the eager anticipation of the little writer.

The Cat Sleep

One day the cat said. I am ging to sleep.
gone to sleep. She went to sleep. By the

time I went to sleep I heard a noise. So
I went to the bed and I look there and
them. I went to the chair and I look there **and**
and them Boo?
  P s ti si a Mouse
the end

Certainly this is a challenge to one's ingenuity. How can one
present such a story as this in a way that will give the child his
bright moment of delight? The teacher chose to read it at the
very beginning of the reading period. With Johnny pressing
warmly against her shoulder, she summoned every ounce of
dramatic ability she had and by her very voice and manner gave
importance to the tale. She turned to beam on the child, saying,
"O, Johnny, our very first riddle story. What fun!" And then
before the other children could sense the obvious inadequacies,
she rushed on to the next story. Johnny went on writing and
each succeeding tale required less agility and drama of his
teacher.

Sometimes the offerings are actually offensive to our taste,
but these, too, we have received without adverse comment. This
may take considerable forbearance, as children can be very
thorough in establishing the tone of a story. Stories about
messes are disgustingly detailed and these, by the way, are always
very humorous (to the children!) ; war stories involve endless
gruesome killings; and many tales are practically dripping with
blood. We have learned to ignore the qualms we may have and
to listen to these distressing themes, if not with enthusiasm, then
at least with courteous attention. This excerpt from "Red
Duke" is a sampling of an epidemic of "tough" stories that
swept a fifth grade.

"So you three mugs thought you'd squeal on Red Duke, eh? Well,
there ain't anyone never squealed on Red Duke that really lived to
tell about it," said Red Duke, breathing hard.
"Aw, let's kill the dirty squealers and get it over with," said Jake
with his finger on his trigger.
"Shut your mouth, I'm running this gang," said Red Duke. "I'll

rub these boys out when I'm ready, see?" He glared at the trembling men. "Now you lily-livered yellow dogs, how much does Black Mike know?"

Even this we took quietly with perhaps no further comment than the truthful one that the rough language and vigorous action are admirably suited to the characters. Older children inevitably recognize our personal likes and dislikes, but by that time their confidence in our genuine interest in every story is well established. A sixth-grader offered his repulsive war story to us with the easy remark, "This isn't the kind of story you like but I knew you would read it. I think it's keen."

There are stories, too, that verge on impertinence. These are always about imaginary beings who, of course, are not bound by the usual rules of decorum. Even so it may rankle to hear a teacher labelled Miss Pastypuss and described as "a nice old gal," or to see one of our own foibles humorously portrayed. However, this is never a personal attack; it is a natural and mild outburst against adults for the sense of inferiority they make youngsters feel.

All children yearn at times " to put grown-ups in their place," and if they write freely, their hidden emotions are bound to show through. So we listen undisturbed to these revealing stories because we know that only by accepting ideas as they are offered can we cultivate the sincerity and fearlessness that we profess to crave.

Mrs. Widdle Waddle Teaches School

One day when Mrs. Widdle Waddle was making her bed, the telephone rang. Then she stopped making her bed and ran to the phone and answered it.

"Hello," said Mrs. Widdle Waddle.

"Hello," said a voice, "I am Mrs. Pickle Puss and I am a school teacher and I am going to go away and visit another school and I was wondering if you would please take my place this morning and I will be back this afternoon."

"Well, all right," said Mrs. Widdle Waddle because she thought she would like it very much. And then Pickle Puss said good-bye and hung up.

"Well," said Mrs. Widdle Waddle, "I am going to like this. I guess I had better not finish my bed but get on my coat and go."

So she got on her coat and locked the door and walked to school. After a while she got to the school and found the children scribbling all over the blackboard and pounding on the piano and messing up her desk.

Mrs. Widdle Waddle said, "Stop it."

The little boys said, "Mind your own business, Madam, will you please?"

Mrs. Widdle Waddle didn't know what to say but rang the school bell. That meant for the children to call the attendance cards. This time the children obeyed her.

"Sammy, Johnny, Jane, Joan, Mary Lou, and Rose," said Mrs. Widdle Waddle. "Well, I guess those three are late and so is Sammy Jay and Mary. Now for Arithmetic."

"Pooh," said all the children. "Recess is what we want." And before she knew it they were out in the court where they played.

"Oh, dear," said Mrs. Widdle Waddle as she walked out into the courtyard. "Children, come here." But instead they threw a football at her and laughed.

"Oh, well," said Mrs. Widdle Waddle not knowing very well what to do and it hurt a little where the football hit her.

"Well," she said, "I'll let you stay out a little longer."

She really wanted to be alone while she had a stomach ache. But she wasn't alone because when she went into the school there were Sammy Jay and Rose and Mary Lou.

Sammy said, "I thought I would be late."

"So did my mother," added Rose and Mary Lou.

"But you are late," said Mrs. Widdle Waddle.

They all looked up in a startled way. "Oh, boo hoo," they all cried at once. "We are late. Boo hoo."

"Oh, well," said Mrs. Widdle Waddle, "I wish Mrs. Pickle Puss would come back." But finally she did come back.

"Well, hello," said Mrs. Pickle Puss. Mrs. Widdle Waddle was so relieved that she got up and said her good-bye and went home.

"Well," said Mrs. Pickle Puss after Mrs. Widdle Waddle had gone, "did you get your Arithmetic O.K. and your Spelling O.K.?"

"Yes, yes," said all the children at once and Sammy Jay added, "No one was late and the Arithmetic and Spelling papers were thrown away because they were all O.K."

"Well, good," said Mrs. Pickle Puss, "good for you."

And at the same time Mrs. Widdle Waddle was saying at home,
"I'll never do that again."

Being sure of the teacher's friendly concern adds immeasurably to the joy of writing a story. Children are often eager to
read the first part of a tale to her; indeed we have known many
who come with shining eyes to show each new paragraph. Still
more often youngsters look up from their writing to say, "Just
wait 'til you read this one." "You'll be crazy about *this* part."
It is easy to tell by the tingle in the voice that every sentence
has added zest because of the prospect of sharing it with an appreciative friend — added zest and added power, too, for joy
releases power just as surely as uncertainty or fear restricts it.

PRESENTATION TO THE CLASS

Delightful as is the enthusiastic acceptance by the teacher,
the truly exciting experience is the presentation of one's story
to the class. A few children may wish to keep their stories
"secret," and we respect their wishes even when it means that
over a period of years we see but a small fraction of their
personal writing. Occasionally, although a child enjoys sharing
his story with his teacher he may hesitate to present it to the
group. Usually the temptation, "I know the class would enjoy
your story, especially the part where. . . . May I read it to them?"
is too strong to resist. However, if he truly does not want his
story read, we never insist.

At the eight-and-nine-year age, youngsters sometimes seek
the assurance of our approval before they offer their stories to
the class. In the early stages we read the tales to the group,
partly because youngsters of this age rarely have enough skill
to read effectively their hastily written and often telegraphic accounts, and partly because we can, through dramatic reading,
bring out the good points and cloak the insufficiencies.

Later, toward the end of third or beginning of fourth grade,
children begin to take over the presentation of their own stories.
In order to achieve the best possible results, the preparation
for this is carefully done. When a story is finished the young

writer goes off by himself into a quiet corner or out into the hall to practice reading aloud so that he can successfully "put his story across" to his audience. He may discover where words have been omitted or where the meaning is not clear, but these rough places can be quickly mended by the insertion of a few words or phrases. This is the time, too, when the perfect title may pop into his head, although as we have previously stated, the naming of a story is not a required step.

We do not underestimate the importance of setting the stage for this sharing occasion. Paying attention to such details as a comfortable and cozy seating arrangement so that the reader does not have to strain to make himself heard, and choosing a time when the class is in a relaxed and receptive mood make possible the full depth of satisfaction children can derive from these experiences. These satisfactions in turn produce the enthusiasm and the impetus that carry story writing on and on.

VALUE OF ORAL PRESENTATION

The frequent periods of reading and listening are a vital part of the writing process. There is no greater spur to writing than the keen delight of watching one's story "catch" an audience, unless perhaps it be the heart-warming approval that follows the reading. Again and again a nine-year-old sits rigid with happiness or twisting excitedly while his story is being read; and then in a sudden burst of sheer joy makes the announcement, "I'm going to write more stories. My next one will be even better'n this one. I bet I write a hundred stories." And often an older child, though more self-contained, is no less moved by the pleasure of his accomplishment. Donna, in the absorbing excitement of her reading, used to wriggle herself halfway across the floor, and sometimes she grew so pleased she laughed aloud.

Although we urge the children to present their own stories simply because they enjoy doing so, we have discovered in the wake of this reading aloud three important values that at first we did not foresee. Oral reading itself has improved. Many children who spoke in dull halting tones when using books, read their own stories in an easy, lively fashion. This gain has held, in part at least, when they return to book reading. Improvement in writing style is a second by-product. Because of the abundance of reading and listening, the tongue and ear have learned to work together to seek for more pleasing sounds, so that the reiterated *and* or *then,* the clumsy connective, the monotonous sentence pattern gradually disappear. Sentences change in length and tempo to fit the changing pace of a story And lastly, the children make headway in recognizing where sentences begin and end. The scribbled papers may be guiltless of capitals and periods and some of the constructions may be rather involved, but a child never fails to read his story correctly. His ear seems to know without question where to stop and start again.

But far more significant than the gains in English power is the effect upon the personality of the child himself. There is something deeply rewarding in the feeling that accompanies the reading of one's own story to a group. Because each creation is unique, because there in black and white is the idea that until now has been an intriguing but invisible part of himself, because each story is woven out of his own being, the glow of success is a peculiarly personal and vitalizing one. It is obvious to an adult that the child unconsciously identifies himself with the protagonist of his tale and accepts as his own the praise and approval accorded his hero. In addition, he is the all-powerful manipulator of all the characters of his story. Briefly he is not a child subject to the limits set by adults, but a being with omnipotent power who moves characters about as he wills. In this dual role of hero and manipulator he stands among his peers as a clever and capable person. Such an experience cannot but add to a child's stature and security. Furthermore, in a world becoming rapidly more mechanized there is little opportunity for a child to know the satisfying experience of identifying himself with his own product. To stand before a group and hold their interest with *his* story awakens in him a sense of innate power and makes him ready for larger ventures.

BLOCKS TO WRITING

Once well initiated, story writing usually continues under its own momentum providing nothing is done to check it. With shy and self-conscious children a very little thing may disturb their confidence and thus shut off the flow of their ideas. Praise or blame can be equally devastating. The former, if excessive, may oppress the sensitive child with the fear that he cannot again equal what he has already done; the latter may but strengthen his conviction that he can't do anything worth while. For this reason evaluation is avoided and interest is kept directed to the way the story affects us, the audience. "Wasn't that part funny or exciting? Couldn't you close your eyes and see Mo coming bumpity-bump down the stairs?"

Sometimes our over-eagerness to be helpful trips us. We have caught ourselves saying, "Jack, that's a wonderful story. Now why don't you. . . ." *It never works!* The child seems to feel that what he is doing is not right, and he promptly puts it aside. It is like the touched egg to which the bird will not return. Such an error makes us realize anew that at this stage our concern lies not so much in the specific product as in the sincerity and on-goingness of the writing process.

In fact we have come more and more to treat each story as an ephemeral thing to be relished and laid aside, and we have turned our eyes expectantly toward new stories. When attention is fixed upon a single narrative a child may come to regard it as a standard or model and try to imitate what he has already done. Others whose writing is not equally lauded may lose faith in their own creations. In a few unfortunate instances certain gifted children have been told their stories were good enough to be published. Immediately self-consciousness set in, and there was a quick falling off in the freshness and vigor of their writing. All of these practices lead, we feel, to stagnation rather than to growth. It is growth that we want — growth that involves the cultivation of spontaneity, the strengthening of the individual voice, and the habit of writing not for commendation, but for the release, the satisfaction, and the power it affords. Therefore we no longer gather stories into more or less permanent booklets nor select "best" stories for school publications. We feel that such activities tend to halt rather than to stimulate growth in writing power. To us it seems better for children to find their reward in the joy of fresh creation rather than in the preserving and revering of what they have already done.

Another effective block to creative effort is over-concern with the clerical aspects of what one is writing. Imagination is a demanding master; it refuses to operate freely when attention is shared with anything else. Since an elementary school child has as yet attained but a small measure of control over the details of English mechanics and form, he must be relieved of responsibility for them if he is to create joyfully and well. Spelling, too, can hamper the flow of ideas, so we promptly give the spelling of any words the children ask for, no matter how simple, because in the excitement of creation many actually forget how to spell even everyday words. No time is used for filing or looking up words in a spelling notebook; good ideas are often lost through such delay. The hardship of writing itself is enough of a deterrent. One has only to watch the tightly held pencil stubbing along to sense the labor involved. As Julie remarked one day, "I just can't keep up with my ideas." And Allen, who is almost a year younger, finds transcription such an ordeal that only every fourth or fifth sentence gets on paper, although he achieves an exciting story even in this fashion.

Once there was a monkey. He was called Minnie, the Monk. One day he was taking a walk through the woods. Then he saw a fire and then he call the fire department. Then he heard a siren. Then he saw the fire truck.

"I rang the bell."

"Where is the fire?"

"This way." (Of course he forgot.) He led them on a wild goose chase.

One fireman said, "Your are going to caught."

"BANG! Bang! BANG!" goes the judge's hammer.

"You are going jail."

"But, but, but, but, but, but, but, but, but, but."

"Shut off your motor boat."

"I saw the fire."

"Well, where is it?"

"I'll find it."

"Come on, boys," says one fireman. "Come on, little monkey."

"Okay, okay, I'm coming." (The fire was right out on the back lawn.)

When Minnie stepped out he saw.

He said, "Fire!"

The firemen ran to the engines.

Indeed, unless we mitigate as much as possible the travail of story writing, the child will not only write fewer stories but shorter, duller ones as well. So it is for this very obvious reason that we have confined our teaching of mechanics to utilitarian writing in which the child is not so emotionally involved. *In personal writing there are never any requirements of form or standards of correctness.*

But the school is not the only influence that can curtail a child's expression. It may be the home that is unwittingly at fault. Tom, who had been writing freely and happily for some time, came to school one day with the troubled announcement, "My mother doesn't think much of the five bears." Now many children in the group had been writing about the bears who had become real and beloved characters. The disparaging remark of Tom's mother, therefore, discredited for him not only his latest story but also the writing of the other children. Tom wrote no more stories that year.

Another child who had begun to write freely was slowed down to a marked degree when his mother belittled his brief but delightful stories by saying, "You're too big to be writing such simple things. When I was your age I could write compositions several pages long." (It is an amusing fact that grown-ups, even when acting in good faith, tend to glorify their own childhood accomplishments.) Pressure to meet an imposed but shadowy standard undermines a child's confidence in his own power and so confuses him that writing ceases to be gratifying and becomes instead a labored effort to satisfy a demand that he doesn't comprehend but feels obligated to meet.

It is unquestionably true that the stories that are created out of a child's own urge to write are more crude and ragged than the tidy compositions of a generation ago. At the same time they are more sincere and they exhibit a far more generous use of good techniques of English expression. This, we feel, is as it should be. The period of elementary school life is primarily one of development through experience and exploration. Crystallizing forms too soon only limits the possibilities of growth. Our object in story writing is to cultivate a sense of joy and power in performing the activity, and we feel that conscious evaluation and improvement of the creative products of this activity should wait for a later period of near-adulthood. Until the desire to write is firmly established, correction and criticism can but halt the whole process.

This explains why, in certain cases, there is a divergence of opinion between the school and the home, and it poses a considerable problem. We have had some successes and some dreadful failures in trying to explain our point of view to parents. When discussing the English program in parents' meetings we mention how differently we approach the two types of writing. To show that we are not neglecting the tried and true English essentials we send home evidences of practical writing, which we require to be accurately and painstakingly done, but we make every effort to keep the carelessly written story papers in our own hands. As we watch the later records of children whom we have taught, we are more and more convinced that the stress we lay on respecting one's own thoughts and expressing them in one's own way pays far richer dividends than are gained through demanding that the clerical aspects of every paper be praiseworthy.

There are always a few children who rarely, if ever, seek the satisfactions to be found in imaginative writing. For them, we depend on practical writing, which is required of all children, to reveal their growing ability to put ideas into words. In reports and articles we take pains to commend any gleam of style or touch of unique expression that may appear. In this way we try to increase their desire to express themselves with vividness and individuality. And beyond this we feel an added obligation to search for and find other avenues for their imaginations to explore. It is essential that all children have some way of pouring out the ideas that are peculiarly theirs. Perhaps in music or rhythms or dramatics, in the sports, the arts, or the sciences, they will realize the delight of evolving something uniquely their own and will feel the spur to further effort that each attempt at creation brings.

Certainly to try to force children to "write for pleasure" dams the whole stream of writing, *both* practical and personal. However, once in a rare, rare while we do try to help even the laggards catch the excitement of storytelling. Our usual way is to take some day when the mood seems right, to gossip about one of our familiar story characters. We all may invent funny things he did when he was little or propose possible future escapades. When ideas begin coming we may say, "Oh, these are fun! For the next fifteen minutes let's write them down as fast as we can." Sometimes we write, too; sometimes we move about the room to give a needed lift to a fearful child. We may play secretary to a slow writer or stop to exclaim over some scrap of fresh invention. The literary results of such an experience are usually of small value but often some sluggish minds are stirred or a few of the diffident discover that they, too, have ideas. This kind of mass stimulation is charily used. For the most part we place no requirement of time or quantity upon personal writing.

HOW CHILDREN WRITE

The infinite variety of human nature is nowhere more apparent than in the strange and sometimes devious ways that children follow in putting thoughts on paper. Some can write in the midst of swirling activity while others find the presence of even one other person a deterrent. Some love notebooks and the snugness of pages between covers; other choose the freeness of single sheets. Some think out all of a story in advance; others work from the most trivial starting point and know only what is going to happen next. Some write best in solitude; others like to write occasionally with a partner.

This desire to write a story with another child at first caused us real concern. Only reluctantly did we give permission for its trial, with many a pedagogical fear that each might not be learning as much as he should. After experimenting for more than a year, we became convinced that a child who sometimes wants to write with a friend, perhaps in a classroom corner or some other protected spot, is really freed and fortified by the experience. One child who had produced very little distinctive writing made up a complicated mystery with two other children. Afterwards he turned quite naturally to writing alone again, and his humorous account of the difficulties of moving from a house to a town apartment was a decided improvement over any previous solo writing.

The excellence that can be achieved by partner writing is clearly evident in the following story written in fifth grade. Two little girls worked so congenially that the product reflects the personal flavor of both and not the dominance of one, as we had feared it might.

In the Land of Ringing Bells

In the Land of Ringing Bells the Mayor was very worried because all of the time he would try to make a speech and the bells would ring. Whenever he would try to listen to the radio the bells would ring. Whenever he would try to talk with the chief of police the bells would ring. The mayor grew disgusted; he grew mad until he grew *furious*. Now the Mayor could not think what to do about these bells so he went away to think without the bells ringing in his ears. While the Mayor of the town was away the people tried to think up a way to stop the bells from ringing but they did not succeed. When the Mayor came back he had thought of a way to stop the bells. He told his followers to tie the clappers with rope and take a bottle of glue to make them more secure. Now the pages got half way up to the bells when they started to ring as loudly as they could. The followers clapped their hands to their ears and ran to the Mayor. He had expected this so he gave his followers six inches of sealing wax to protect their ears from the sound. The followers put the wax in their ears. They went up to the bells again and succeeded in tying the clappers. Now all this happened on Sunday morning when everyone was in church. The priest was supposed to let the people out at twelve o'clock but it was now three. The priest feared that if he let the people out before the bells rang twelve he would be arrested by the chief of police. The cooks all came running down the street looking for their mistresses. When they heard that they were in church they reported it to the police. The police arrested the priest. The people went home to eat their cold dinner. Now this sort of thing went on all through the week until the people of the town complained to the Mayor. So finally the Mayor made a proposition to the bells to ring only when they were needed. And the bells kept their promise.

This is but one of many stories written by pairs or trios. Without exception we have been pleasantly surprised by their quality and sparkle. Our fear that in such combinations one worked and the other loafed has been completely dispelled. Indeed, it appears that here as elsewhere, ideas grow in the company of ideas.

Then again, some children work slowly, laboriously choosing each word and achieving an economy of expression. Others write quickly and with a flourish, dashing off a story as fast as a pencil can go. Still other children write a bit, erase, rewrite, cross out, start over, and finally out of an assortment of scribbled scraps with arrows, erasures, and patches fashion an appealing story that delights the group.

There seems to be no limit to the ways of writing needed by different personalities. Each is uniquely appropriate to the person who thus expresses himself, and any inclination to change a child's own way of writing should be firmly checked.

THE UNFINISHED STORY

Not every story reaches the stage of completion necessary for reading aloud. Many times a child abandons a story half finished, and rightly so. Invention is at best a fickle power. A child may start a story in a fine burst of enthusiasm only to find that his idea doesn't work out and his invention dwindles; the adventure that had begun so gaily comes to a standstill, and he is heartily disappointed in it. Now one might say that the thing to do is to require him to finish it, to insist that this story be completed before another is started. Upon a few fatal occasions we, with a puritanical eye on character building, have followed this policy. Almost without exception the children have tied trite conclusions to their often delightful beginnings. Nothing has been gained but a salute to perseverance. Nothing has been gained and much has been lost. The forced completion has made all story writing such a disagreeable experience that only a singularly courageous child again attempts a venture that might so suddenly turn into painful drudgery. The teacher is left with a complete but woefully unbalanced story and the serious problem of overcoming a child's distaste for writing.

There are many times when a story is best left half finished. Often the beginning is so engaging that it is difficult to accept the child's verdict, "I don't like it any more." "I don't know how to end it." "I have a better idea now." Here for instance is Ann's story. It starts in a pleasing manner, but it is easy to detect the spot where her invention faltered.

Once upon a time there lived a great big hen. She had laid some eggs. She was just going to sit on them when she saw a big fat worm. "Well," she thought, "this will be my last time I go off my nest. One little worm won't hurt."

But sly Mr. Fox was close by in the branbles. "My two dear children like eggs. I think I will get them some," he said. So went home half-walking and half-running. He told his children how long it had been since they had some nice, soft-boiled eggs.

"May I have that ball, the little one you were playing with yesterday?"

"Here it is," said one of the foxes. "But you have spoiled our little ball."

"Do you want eggs?" said the fox. "Do you want to play a joke on Mrs. Hen?"

"Yes," was the reply.

"Now," he said, "which one of you wants to go to the beach with me?" They all did so Mr. Fox took them all.

When they got to the beach Mr. Fox told them to wait on the sand. Then he took the rubber ball and went down to the ocean and filled it with sea water. He then took his children home to bed. The next day he got up bright and early and again hid in the bushes near Mrs. Hen's house. Now Mrs. Hen saw. . . .

Ann said, "I'm sick of this story — it's flopped." We agreed. Better to drop the story there, having had the fun of inventing Mrs. Hen and Sly Fox than to drag it to a lifeless close. We accepted Ann's verdict quietly and read with enjoyment what she had written. Thus we kept the way open for future stories, many of which reached a conclusion satisfactory to Ann.

At other times it is obvious that a youngster has written a part of a story just for the fun of using a word or phrase that has excited his imagination. Having used the bewitching phrase, he has no further interest in the story and is content to drop it. Here is a nine-year-old's unfinished tale plainly written just to use a fascinating word.

The king was in an awful rage. "Where is my wise councillor?" he shouted.

"Here I am, your majesty," said the wise councillor, bowing until his beard touched the floor.

"Well, don't I have the biggest castle in all the world?" said the king.

"Indubitably, your majesty," said the wise councillor, bowing until his beard touched the floor.

"And don't I have the largest army in the world?"

"Indubitably, your majesty."

"And don't I have the most golden treasure in all the world?"

"Indubitably, your majesty."

"Then why don't I have . . ."

Again a story may be laid aside merely because a newly discovered idea is so tempting that a child loses interest in his
current plot. We have found it wise to let him shift to the fresh
idea since we know that the satisfaction of reading a whole story
will help offset a tendency to skip endlessly from one unfinished
tale to another. The child who regularly abandons his stories,
almost without exception, fails to complete work of other kinds
as well. The basic problem can be better handled in areas in-
volving objective materials than in this realm of highly personal
ideas.

We have learned to value that first quick surge of a story idea
and to hide our disappointment when a promising beginning is
forsaken for a new plan. Occasionally a child returns to an
unfinished story and completes it, but more often he forgets it
in the onrush of new ideas.

Probably one of the most common reasons for not completing
a story is the simple and seemingly unavoidable factor of
physical fatigue. Again and again we have seen a child tire of
his story just because the labor of getting the words on paper
was too onerous. When it is possible to relieve this impasse
by writing for the child from dictation, his interest does not
flag. But this course is seldom feasible.

We do not know to what extent this element of physical
fatigue curbs a child's outpouring of ideas. We do know that
Debby, who writes with average facility for a nine-year-old, spent
five writing periods on a long but never finished story and then
turned to a shorter one. Obviously her loss of interest in the
first was due to fatigue induced by the effort of trying to write
in pace with her swift imagination. We have watched children
who write slowly develop terse, telegraphic styles in order to
transfer their ideas to paper without too great expenditure of
energy. Others have said, "Sure I have a story idea, but I just
thought I would rest this period." Still others have written part
of a story and then, as their hands grew weary, asked to tell the
balance. Some have attached abrupt and trite endings to their
tales, saying in explanation, "I know the ending's not so good

but I got tired writing." This whole matter of fatigue is one aspect of the writing situation about which we are especially curious for we feel it has not yet been adequately examined or dealt with.

TEACHING TECHNIQUES

Abundance of writing is our initial goal, for it is only by writing and writing and writing that the channels of personal communication are opened so that true thinking and feeling come through. We make of our story-writing a kind of play-time — play in the valid sense of being something which one does with one's whole heart — and we do all we can to keep alive the spirit of adventure and fun. As a result we get quantities of stories, many of which are poor and all of which could be improved. Yet we waste no time in remaking the poor ones nor in dwelling overlong on the few that hold promise. It is not the spirit of judgment, but that of spontaneous enjoyment which we wish to maintain. Like the lumbermen around their campfire guffawing over a new Paul Bunyan yarn or the eager crowd transported by a minstrel into knightly feats of derring-do, we, too, ask only to be excited or amused. We feel no need to criticize. When attention is thus focussed on the enchantment of the story and not upon its shortcomings, self-consciousness begins to drop away, and children come, more and more, to find satisfaction and release in the stories they create.

The more they write, the more they must bestir their minds for new ideas. Invention is indeed the primary activity of creative power. It is the *quality* in stories for which we watch most eagerly and which we are quick to acclaim: "That was a different idea." "What a surprise to have Mother Bear . . . ." "You could have ended your story there, but instead you invented another happening. That's good." By question and comment we direct attention to the new, the individual, the unexpected. Such concern may not make for immediate story improvement; but we are working for awakened minds and at the same time we are trying to forestall a rehash of current radio and television fare. We want children to write out of their own musings and reactions, and when they do that, there is always at least a touch of the unique and the unusual.

During the reading periods we watch for such storytelling techniques as may appear, and we try, without seeming to teach, to make the children aware of them also. After a particularly tempting beginning we may stop the reader just long enough for the listeners to realize how much they want him to go on. We do not urge the use of such elements as good beginnings, details of characterization, moments of suspense; because when children are writing with affectionate interest these things begin to appear of their own accord, and this is especially true if they have been mentioned approvingly in other stories. Naturally the effective techniques appear first in the stories of the more imaginative children, but in time others gradually absorb and use them. Each child seems to take over the elements that fit the maturity of his own thinking; hence they are part of the fabric of his story and not something superficially added because he was urged to do so.

Even in matters of vocabulary we no longer stress the use of colorful words. Instead our emphasis is on clear and true imagining; for when a child lives his story vividly in his mind, the fitting words seem miraculously to appear. We appreciate the words, to be sure, but in terms of the effect they have upon us. We see "the little bears squirming in their hot collars"; we hear Nig when he "growled in his toughest voice"; we get the tactile sensation as did Mo when "hesitatingly he touched the baby's soft little paw." There is no special virtue in long words, new words, or bookish words. A word is good only if it tells exactly what the author had in mind.

But far more potent than our guidance, if that can be called guidance which *follows* rather than *precedes,* is the subtle communication between the reader and his audience. The pleased sigh that follows a good beginning says more clearly than any words, *"Now* we're off to a good start." The sharp intake of breath, the irrepressible giggle, the sudden stillness that comes from tense expectancy all tell the reader what grips and moves his hearers. These flashes of success work powerfully to illuminate and foster sound narrative techniques because they are part and parcel of those moments when a story is working its magic in the hearts and minds of those who receive it. Thus against the natural reaction of responsive listeners the children shape and test their story-making power.

Sometimes it is possible to trace to the reading and appreciation of one story the adoption of a specific technique by many of the class. In an eight- nine-year-old group, three quarters of the stories ended with the comfortable and hackneyed assurance, "And they . . . he . . . she lived happily ever after." The other quarter took the hero safely home, gave him his supper and left him in bed. But Mary's story was different.

A Caught Fish

Once there was a little boy. His name was Bob. He was six years old. He decided to go fishing. So he dug some angleworms and got his pole, his fishing pole, and went to a lake. He fished and fished and fished. With angleworms. But he didn't catch anything and he got discouraged. Suddenly a gull flew over his head. The gull squawked and Bob looked up and the gull dropped a fish he was carrying home. Bob caught the fish in his hands. "Well," he said, "at least I can say I caught a fish."

When the teacher finished reading there was a quick outburst of enthusiasm for the swift and dramatic ending:

"Oh, Mary, you stopped right at the place for laughing."

"Well, he *did* catch a fish and that's that."

"In this story the last part is the best of all."

So the story was immediately reread with special emphasis given to the ending.

Although no further discussion of this technique took place, the stock endings soon began to disappear as the children experimented with other conclusions. Two or three wrote obvious imitations of Mary's tale in an effort to capture for themselves the warm approval that had been accorded her. And warm approval they received though not for the imitation, which the children dismissed with "The end sounds like Mary's story," but for some phrase or situation that was really fresh and genuine. Others adapted the technique to fit and strengthen their own styles. Here are the last bits of three stories written shortly after Mary's "A Caught Fish."

The prince came tiredly around the curve of the world back again to his own home and there in the garden with flowers all around it was the golden crown just where he had dropped it.

He went down a long black hall and came to a great door. He pushed and pushed. It finally creaked open. He found himself in *another* big room. "My," he thought, "I'll never get out of here." Just then he saw a window with a water pipe going by it. He quickly rushed to the window, slid down the pipe and was safe at last.

Buttercup Wilkins slowly licked the jam from her face and paws. She carefully closed the door of the jam closet and wearing a smile at the edge of her whiskers she slipped past all the mean chattering cats whose noses were so uppity they did not even see her.

Mary's story alone does not account for this development, but Mary's story *plus* the lively appreciation of it was directly responsible for the experimentation that followed. When children listen constructively to both story and comment, thus identifying themselves with the very warp and woof of the tale and its quality, they become increasingly imbued with what makes writing effective, and inevitably this learning is reflected in their own stories. Appreciative listening sharpens the urge for more writing and deepens the insight necessary for better writing. Indeed, listening, like writing and reading, is an indispensable arc of a productive circle.

ENRICHING ACTIVITIES

Not only do we permit and encourage abundant writing, but we strive to enrich that inner consciousness from which personal expression springs. At odd moments we take time to savor the qualities of things: the stinging drive of rain, the first faint mist of green upon the trees, the muffled sound of footsteps upon a snowy day. We take time, too, to recognize the graphic truth of those spontaneous comments that children often make about what they touch or hear or see.

At times apart from writing periods we share with them some of the beauty, the wonder, the laughter, the ruggedness and vigor that we have found in literature. No medium is its equal for stretching and strengthening the imagination. The atmosphere of our reading is one of warmth and companionship. Here, too, when the action of a story grows lively we may close our eyes to see it better; or we may say together some familiar lines of poetry because we like their meaning or their sound. Nowadays, when through movies, radio, comics, and television children are exposed to so much that is commonplace and artificial, we feel a double obligation to give them satisfying experiences in good literature; else how will many of them know the magic and the rhythm and the power of their mother tongue? Such reading is never consciously compared with the children's own efforts, but we are confident that through their joyous listening much good is absorbed — good that will become part and parcel of that inner store from which the child creator draws.

GAINING CONTROL OF SKILLS

Whether or not there would be satisfactory improvement when children wrote just for the joy of creating a tale was a question that gave us considerable concern when we started our experiment. We can now answer with an unqualified affirmative. In both mechanics and style, the ability of these children at fifth- and sixth-grade levels definitely surpasses that of any other groups we have ever had. We had anticipated growth in the techniques of storytelling, but we were frankly surprised by the extent to which the mechanics taught through practical writing have transferred to personal writing.

It must be remembered that in personal writing there is no

requirement of form; no comment is ever made on correctness or the lack of it; no checking or copying is done. Yet after a lapse of weeks or even months, depending on the individual child, the items of punctuation, paragraphing, capitalization, and spelling taught through practical writing begin to appear in their stories. Even such stumbling blocks as apostrophes and quotation marks, first encountered in utilitarian writing and then explained and checked in that field over a period of time, begin to be used voluntarily in personal writing.

Here we have reproduced a story exactly as Claire in the sixth grade wrote it. It is a fair illustration of the carry-over of forms learned in practical writing. Claire neither asked for nor received help of any sort. Indeed, there was nothing to be gained by correctness, for after the story was read to the class it was put immediately into her folder.

It was Tuesday afternoon and a council was being held in Nig's room. It was being held because the new girl, Jean, who had come to school had invited Roy Bear to supper the night before.

"I say that Eenie's desk should be on one side of her and my desk should be on the other side of her," said Nig.

"But I always get people to like *me*," said Mo.

"You aren't quick enough about it," said Meinie, "it took you four years to get Alice bear to like you and *she's* no good."

"Oh yes she is," said Mo. "As a matter of fact I'm taking her to the movies tonight."

"Well *I'm* taking *Sue* Bear to the movies," said Eenie.

"I'm taking Nellie Bear," said Meenie.

"I'm taking Daisy Mae because Mommy said I could," said Meinie. Poor Nig wasn't taking anyone to the movies so he ran upstairs to his bedroom to hide. Soon he heard the others getting ready to go to the movies and after a while the house was quiet so Nig quietly opened the door and went down stairs to make sure nobody was home. Then he ran to the telephone and just as he got there it rang.

He lifted the receiver and said, "Hello, who is this?"

"It's Jean," said the voice, "could I speak to Nig?"

"This is Nig, what do you want?"

"I want to know if you can go to the movies with me?"

"S-s-s-*sure*," he said and hung up. He ran up stairs and quickly got dressed. Using some of Mother's perfume to fix his hair. He ran down stairs, out the door, and over to Jean's house.

Jean was waiting for him and had telephoned for a taxi. They rode to the movie house and were just ready to get their tickets when Nig realized that he didn't have any money. He started to apologize to Jean when up walked Meinie. He handed Daisy Mae to Nig, took Jean by the hand and got their tickets. Nig was so relieved he didn't mind having Meinie take Jean to the movies and the next day in school he changed his desk with Meinie's.

What has happened is that a reasonable degree of correctness has become a *natural* part of Claire's writing. It is paradoxical that although she corrected a mistake in punctuation in the fourth quotation by placing a period after "Mo" and a capital *A* in *As,* she has let the same type of error pass unnoticed in the preceding quotation. This irregularity is a characteristic step toward automatic control of items of mechanics. From the point of view of form the story is not perfect, but the consistently accurate use of apostrophes, the spelling of such words as *receiver, apologize,* and *relieved,* the generally correct use of punctuation marks and capitals, all point to a real competence. We have, we believe, developed an acceptable degree of power over mechanics by teaching forms in practical writing, and waiting for their inevitable adoption in personal writing.

The illustrations that appear throughout this book give ample evidence of the growth in story-writing ability achieved by our children. What they cannot show is the children's keen delight in their stories, the carefully paced dramatic reading of each adventure, the sidewise glance to see if a special detail has caught the imagination of the audience, the quick lift of shining eyes at the end of the reading to measure the story's appeal. Writing is fun, and when it is fun one writes to renew his own pleasure.

Tell me, where is fancy bred,
Or in the heart, or in the head?
How begot, how nourished?
— WILLIAM SHAKESPEARE, The
Merchant of Venice

5. *Children's Verse*

THUS far we have dealt with several ways in which children
impart their ideas, either through writing or through the
oral exchange that makes way for writing. We have described
how they enlarge and share their understandings in practical
situations. We have indicated how we give them opportunities
for casual conversation, which is a natural and desired outcome
of their being together. And we have told how we welcome and
encourage their innate love of storytelling.

But we have not yet discussed how we try to help children
reveal through language their personal reactions to experience.
To a young child life is new and full of flavor, and he reaches
out to encompass it through all his senses. Because his acquaintance with language is new also, his use of it tends to be original.
Frequently, too, his expression is so vivid and rhythmical that
it verges on poetry.

Unfortunately, many adults seize upon such unusual remarks

122

to quote them as amusing or quaint, or to make them over into a more familiar pattern by saying, "Oh, you mean ———." All too soon a child begins to discount his natural, unique mode of expression and to substitute for it the empty, ready-made phrases that adults put into his mouth and mind. Thus he learns early that commonplace words and ideas protect him so that his own thoughts and feelings will not be laughed at or criticized. Perhaps, and we believe that this is true, they lead him into having commonplace thoughts and feelings as well. The fresh insight, the vivid emotion, the sensitive awareness wither away, and the original quality of language begins to disappear. So it is that children lose touch with the deep core of their own individuality. Happily, this contact can be restored — at least in part. They can be led again to savor experiences more poignantly, and to enjoy telling their reactions to them. Although their comments may not be poetry, for want of a better term we call them so, and undoubtedly they are the stuff out of which poetry is made.

EARLY EXPERIENCES IN POETRY

Nature phenomena seem to lend themselves readily to the adventure of poetry telling. We all are affected consciously or subconsciously by stars, night, changes in the season's, the winter's cold, the color of autumn; but we forget that these experiences are not timeworn to children.

Perhaps, when there is a heavy fog or when the first frost covers the ground, we talk about it together, and the children are encouraged to put into words their awareness of the miracle. They react keenly to the quiet of fog, the sheen of a frost-covered lawn, the clink of icy branches, the sound of snow crunched under foot. Looking at these out-of-door happenings closely often establishes a mood in which they tap hidden resources of thought and feeling.

One windy morning the children came in drenched by an unexpected storm. They were so excited by the experience that they were talking breathlessly about what it was like. Each child seemed to be searching for the exact words to describe how it affected him. We said, "Let me write down what you're saying about the storm. It may paint a picture or be a make-believe idea or tell something you wonder about. You don't have to say much — just a few words that really fit can do the trick. You'll have to keep very quiet inside so that you won't scare away your thoughts."

And then as they sat on the floor close to the teacher, there came a quiet, expectant waiting, which gradually gave place to open delight as they took turns telling their ideas. We wrote feverishly in an effort to capture them all. Of course, there was time afterward to read aloud what they had said, and to savor it. Here are some of their thoughts about the storm:

> The wind has a shape like the waves.
>
> It is pushing through the trees
> It has holes in it so it can get by
>   the branches.
>
> The wind is rustling through the grasses
> It is whistling down the valleys.
>
> The wind is sweeping through the town
> It is resting on the housetops.
>
> The wind sounds like a boat
> Leaving the dock.
>
> It sounds like fairies
> Whispering to each other.
>
> It is raining needles
> Because it pricks you —
> It's like a porcupine
> Rubbing against you.
>
> Clouds open up
> And swiftly little drops come down.
>
> The rain touches the blades of grass
> And they bend with the heavy load.

> I think that the sky and ground
> Look like they were twins —
> The puddles look like the grey sky
> And they look so much alike
> That I think that it's hard
> To tell them from each other.

Often we have stimulated our classes to poetic effort by reading to them from our collection of child-made poems. Through hearing the ideas of other children they become more aware of their own thoughts and feelings, and hence they respond more creatively to the writing of their peers than they do to that of adults. Of course, we read an abundance of other poetry, too, but we do it at times when they are not engaged in expressing their own ideas.

Reading aloud periods are very short. They take place when the class is relaxed and comfortable. During the reading we may mention a part that "sounded different" or "was a new way of talking about rain, or snow, or fog" or that used picture words. Only a little reading and talking is done each time. Ten minutes when the group is really quiet and listening is a far better investment than a longer stretch when they are not so receptive.

On these occasions we usually avoid material that rhymes because a child's ear often is so captured by the rhyming that he misses the meaning and the individual voice. When he tries to make poems of his own, he is likely to forget his ideas and concentrate on the jingle.

Our choice of poems, like the following, is a careful one, and here, too, we take advantage of children's wonder in the natural world about them.

> Morning is when the sun
> Wakes up.
> He yawns
> And turns his lantern on.
> He wakes up all the birds
> And other animals, too.

I surely would hate to be the sun
Getting up so early
In the morning.
I've never gotten up
Before him.
I wonder how he knows
What time it is.
I guess the moon comes in
And stops to wake him up
Before he goes on
To night again.

The moon must get tired
Of his business
Because on rainy nights
He never comes out.
That must mean
He's taking a snooze
Under the white clouds.
The stars crowd in with him —
He goes rolling out
Because he has no room.
After he rolls out
He mumbles to himself,
"How greedy those little stars are —
They can rest all the time
When I have to sit
Up in my throne
And shine upon the earth."

The wind comes down
In braids;
It comes down
Twirling around
On the clouds
When they're low.
The rain comes down
In splatters.

I like to watch the wind go by —
It must get out of breath.
I wonder how it floats

And ruffles
And makes all that noise
Many times at night
It wakes me up
With all its tumbling.

In the springtime the earth wears a cloak
Of green velvet,
But in the winter time
The green cloak turns to white;
And the people on the earth
Make it look like it is soiled and spotted.

The cars are rolling along the snow-dressed road
Looking like black bugs — softly, softly
Horns honk in the grey mist — softly, softly
As the snow drifts down
Softly, softly.

Darkness creeps along
As if it were going to pounce upon you.
On rainy days he steals the sun.
The clouds come floating by —
The darkness must run its fastest
To get to the other side of the world.

When the silver raindrops
Softly patter on the earth
It sounds like small feet running along,
And the trees hold out their arms
To catch the gleaming.

Children enjoy, too, poems that give make-believe reasons or
paint vivid pictures.

One time I was out on a fine summer day
With my father and my brother.
We were picking flowers, lovely wild forget-me-nots.
The sun was shining brightly.
I saw a nice white cloud in the sky.
Then pelt, pelt, pelt —
Shower drops fell down.
When I got home I made puddles on the floor
Just like a snowman in the house.

The little grasshopper
Glides from one grass blade
To another
As though he were trying
To commit suicide
By falling on a sword.
He doesn't seem to have much luck
But he hasn't come
To poison ivy yet.

Where does the dark go?
I don't know.
It may go down the well
And have the wind pull it up
In buckets.
Or it may go down the chimney to hide,
And then when he thinks
The day has been enough
He creeps out.
All of a sudden,
Before you know it,
It's dark.
I do wonder where the dark goes.

Pansies nod their faces
In the breeze
Gossiping the news
Of a new little baby
That was born.
He has a velvet face, all yellow with violet,
And his mother is so proud.
That's the gossip that goes around
When a new pansy baby is born.

Tinfoil crinkles,
Glass cracks — then breaks.
Tin sings its song
On the pantry shelf
All day.

The world goes around so fast —
And don't forget
It goes upside down, too.
I don't know why
I don't fall off
On my ear
When it's upside down.
And when I reach the end
I hope I don't have to jump
Very far.

The wind is dashing
Through the trees;
It knocks the poor little leaves
Off their hinges
And chases them down
To the ground.
And then the mean old wind
Whisks them into the fire
Where they burn
Into black crumbly ashes.

   Some of the poems we read are those that divulge secret
thoughts and longings — those thoughts that little children tell
when they are not yet afraid of being misunderstood or laughed
at. Even though these expressions may have no intrinsic poetic
worth, they do have therapeutic value, for often they are dictated by shy, insecure children, who, through the telling, gain
faith in themselves.

CHILD POEMS FOR READING ALOUD

Whenever I'm in trouble
And talk to myself out loud
The trees nod their heads
To and fro —
They know what is troubling me;
They hold out their arms
As if to make a bed for me.

I've always hated little children
Younger than me
Because they have
Such funny ideas.
They always want
To play with dolls and things.
That isn't a bit like me —
I always like to pretend
I'm a mother
And can drive a car.
I wish they were like me
Sometimes at least.

I wonder why birds
Sing so beautifully
Maybe it's because they practice
Or maybe it's because
They were born to know how.

Where do you get your brown fur
Teddy Bear?
How come your soft brown fur
Is so nice
And comfortable?
If I go to sleep with you
Do you mind
The rolling over you I do —
You still are so comfortable?

My dog is furry all over —
His nose is pink,
His eyes are small and round.
He looks like a big snowflake
With fur sticking out.
He sort of smiles in a way.
I take him up in my arms
And pat him.

I'm sick and tired
Of snow —
Not *one* day
Of green grass!

Home's left behind when I go away traveling.
All my dolls as children may come with me,
But still my house is left behind.
My dogs and animals all may come,
But home is left behind.

When I wrap my baby tooth
As tight as I can
In some paper
I put it under my pillow
Quietly
And go to sleep.
That same night
I reach under
And pull out the tooth
Hoping there'd be a surprise.
I would find
My same old tooth there
That the fairy has decided
Not to come that night.
I was twitching
And rolling and boiling
Because I didn't have a surprise.

Feathers tickle.
Why don't they tickle
The hen?
They're on his back
So I think
They should tickle him —
They tickle ME.

I love to go out riding
But last Sunday
When we went out riding
There were six people
In the car
And that meant
I had to sit up front
Between my brother
And my Daddy.
I didn't mind it at all

Except I wished my Daddy
Wouldn't buy my brother
Such scratchy pants
And the candy
Was forever in the back seat
Not in the front
Where it should be.

April is a month
When all the flowers
Come popping
Out of the ground.
It is just like a warning
That summer's coming.
All the flowers
Show their little buds
And so do the trees.
Even the grass
Shows happiness
By filling up your lawn
With its greenness.
April is a special month
Just for loveliness.

I always wondered
If cocoons were butterflies,
I always wondered
How they creep out of their shells,
I always wondered
How they creep along,
I never could see their feet.
I think they do very well
For their age and how small they are.
I wonder how they learned how to fly —
I think they taught themselves.
Sometimes I wonder if I could fly
As well as they could.

A giant shadow
Is what makes the dark.
The giant is after an old man.
The old man has gotten away

From the giant
Once before
But he won't get away again.
The moon is the giant's light
Hunting for the old man.
Every night you see the light.
The man lives out in some woods
He's very poor
No one lives around there.
There is a brook that goes
Right by his house.
He never dares to go out
Because there is a clearing
Out there
And the moon can see it.

We've got a Japanese cherry tree
That grows in our back yard.
It glows with pink
And makes a background
For all the other things —
Like a candle in the corner.

At night
When I go to bed
You never would know
What's going inside my mind;
But it's nice to think
About all sorts of things
That nobody would know about
Except yourself.
I think and think
And when I wake up
In the morning
You would never know
That I thought about
Those things
And *I* even don't know;
But the next night
I try to remember
And keep the same adventure.

POETRY-MAKING BEGINS

Sometimes early in the reading, sometimes late, children begin making poems of their own. Since the ideas often are fleeting, they may be lost before a child can write them down. Therefore, provision must be made for him to dictate them.

At the outset of a poetry-making period we take time to get the group in tune for it. We read a few carefully selected poems to create an appropriate mood and we talk a little to help them get started. We may say something like this: "Telling a poem is like painting a picture, only it's painting with words. It's as if you were standing by pots of paint and splashing the color on a paper with rapid strokes before the picture could leave your mind. A story comes more slowly. It has more words and often starts with 'Once upon a time.' But when you tell a poem you plunge right in, and with just a few words you give a picture or a feeling or a make-believe reason for something."

Another time we remarked, "Poems sometimes tell your hidden feelings. Try telling about your wonderings or your secret wishes."

For a few very shy youngsters the following comments seemed to open the way: "Making up poems is like water flowing from a spring that has been choked up. First it is muddy, but after it has flowed for a while, the water bubbles forth clear and sparkling. You'll find that it's exciting to tell poems. You never know when you are going to get something you'll especially like. So you have to keep on letting them pour out."

We often suggest: "A good time to think of poetry ideas is at night just before you go to sleep when you have that comfortable drowsy feeling."

By stressing the fact that poetry is a quick way of saying something — "Poems don't need all the words that are put into stories; you just hit the high spots" — children are helped to make the transition from the detailed wordiness of a story to the essence-like quality of poetic expression.

The room setting is extremely important. The children and the teacher, too, should feel free from pressure. Quietness and a minimum of movement are two essentials. Before dictation begins, we help the children start activities on which they can work alone. Painting or crayoning a picture, modeling with clay, or weaving will keep the hands busy and at the same time permit the child's mind to follow any course it chooses. Not all are active. Some find that sitting in a quiet corner, or looking out of the window helps them to reach that dreamy state in which their thoughts take on the feeling of poetry.

We usually sit at a low table beside the one who is dictating. The table is purposely low, for even the physical set-up must not conspire to place the teacher in a dominating position. Because the presence of another is often confusing, each child comes up by himself to tell his poem. If, while he is dictating, others have poetry ideas, they raise their hands and we jot down their names. As soon as possible, we call them in turn.

At the close of a period of poetry dictation we read at least one contribution from each child who has participated. We do the reading to give the poems the best possible oral treatment. Thus every child has the satisfaction of hearing his ideas read aloud. At the same time his attention is directed toward those parts that have individual flavor. Here is one way of doing this: When all of the poems have been read, we let the children tell which parts made them see pictures or were new ways of telling something that is true. Interestingly enough, it is the worth-while things they mention. The mediocre expressions have not made sufficient impression to be remembered.

To free children so that they can reveal their interior thoughts is a matter that calls for patience and faith on the part of the teacher. She listens carefully for each hint of the individual voice and she welcomes it warmly, no matter how crude it may be. Indeed, it is the crude expression that often tells of superior things to come. The glib or sentimental phrases are a far cry from the honest, unaffected responses of the real child person.

Their first feeble efforts must meet with reassurance if children are to learn to accept their own way of saying things. No child can have faith in himself unless he is confident that his clumsy attempts will be graciously received with no suggestions for changes or improvements, and no belittling comments by other members of the class.

Of course, the opening-up process takes time and at first yields only meager results. But slowly, as children gain the courage to be themselves, there is a deepening of sensitivity coupled with a growing ease of communication, until eventually many of them attain the power to reveal their sincere reactions in language that is fitting and poetic.

From the beginning the emphasis is on letting children respond easily and naturally to experience. There has to be time for "moodling" if they are to discover that "down underneath" they have thoughts that will surprise and please them. We avoid showing undue concern about the words they use, for we know that when ideas and feelings are welling up spontaneously the right words to express them will come. We may comment casually on the fact that such words as *pretty, nice, beautiful, lovely* tell little; however, we never let a piece of real poetry pass by without taking pains to appreciate it. For example, we point out how clearly one can hear the sound of the wind when Lois says, "It wakes me up with all its tumbling"; or can see the blowing storm clouds when John says, "The clouds are mad, they are bursting with madness." We share our delight in Bob's vivid image of the Japanese cherry tree, which "glows with pink and makes a background for all the other things — like a candle in the corner."

POETRY WITH PRIMARY CHILDREN

It is fascinating to discover that even very young children take pleasure in dictating their poetry ideas. The following groups of poems, told by six- and seven-year-olds, illustrate the growth in self-expression that occurred over a two-year period. A few of their first attempts are given to show how very simple were the beginnings of this poetry dictation. In the second group are poems that were dictated later on in the first and second grades.

Leaves, I love you
When you are colored.

Raindrops, raindrops,
Come and give your patter
On the roof.

Sunshine, sunshine,
I wish you would sunshine
All through the spring.

Come little snowflake,
Come little snowflake,
Soon it will be
Good time to play.

These were dictated later in the first and second grades:

Moon, moon,
I seem as if I could ride in you
Like a sailboat.
You are so beautifully like a princess
You should have diamond clothes.
In the dark you shine like fire.

Little tree
Standing still
He sees everybody
Standing still.

Oh, the sailboats
Floating down the river
And the steamboats and the freight boats
Puffing down the big, big lake
Puff — chug! Puff — chug!

Sunshine,
I like you.
Would you come for a big while
Because I want to make a picture of you?
I shall color the sky
Just as yellow as you are.

One time I got to China
I heard the bangs and noise.
When I pulled my head back in
I never dug again.

Puff, puff —
The trains go
Up the tracks and down the tracks,
Carry people and baggage
Up the tracks and down the tracks,
All the day through —
Puff, puff.

I wonder why
You look so pretty
I want to know, Christmas tree.
Is it because
You bounce so softly
And you break?
The Christmas tree
Could not answer.
All it could do
Was jingle against itself.
The little star
On the top of the tree
Could not answer either;
He could only move around.
Pretty Christmas tree!

When I'm in New York
All I see is crowds —
Some going in theaters
Some going down the street
Some going in offices.
In the night
I see elevator lights:
The buildings light up,
They look like fireflies
Anchored in the air.

Little birdie,
Every winter do you go down south?
'Cuz Mommie's going down
In the great big car;

If you stay on top of it
You can fly tomorrow morning.

When I'm at my father's office
There's nothing to do
It bores me
All there is to do
Is cut out paper things
And throw them
Off the fire escape.
It used to be fun
When the baby pigeons
Were there.
Now it's so drowsy
Waiting for my mother
To pick me up —
Nothing to do
But talk to the shoeshine man
While he shines my father's shoes.
That's not fun
Just sitting
Doing nothing
Most of the time.

FURTHER SUGGESTIONS FOR TEACHERS

In a busy schoolroom poetry-making does not go on without interruption. Because it requires an atmosphere that is singularly free from pressures it cannot flourish when children are engrossed in other types of class activity, such as preparing a program or following a strong science or social studies interest. But in those unhurried periods that afford a sense of leisure and repose, poetry-making can come into its own. After dictation gets under way it is well to continue it for at least a week or two even at the cost of considerable readjustment of the daily schedule. Poetry-making is essentially an uncovering process, and the truly personal thoughts and feelings are often slow to emerge. However, as children begin to realize the satisfaction that comes from voicing their own ideas, they unconsciously permit more and more of their deeper selves to be revealed. Often they become so captivated by the experience that they appear before school begins in the morning or stay on after dismissal to have their poems written down.

Even the best child poems contain only a line or two of unusual beauty or individual sparkle, and in an effort to create a more perfect whole a teacher may feel tempted to weed out ordinary expressions or to build up worthwhile bits. It is well to remember that it is just as dishonest for an adult to change a child's utterances as it is for a child to copy the work of another and call it his own. Moreover, a child is bound to suffer loss of confidence when a teacher makes suggestions for the improvement of a poem, or adds a few words to smooth over what she considers to be the rough spots.

Much of the satisfaction that children derive from poetry-making comes when their ideas are read aloud to the class. It is this sharing that seems to insure the on-goingness of the experience. When a poem is especially colorful or original in its expression of truth, it receives appreciative comments from the others, but it is never unduly featured. Once it has been shared with the group its maker seems to forget about it. Instead of mulling over what has been done, he turns instinctively to new effort. The publishing of an unusual poem in the school magazine or newspaper so focuses the spotlight of attention on it that it takes on the characteristics of a model. Often the child who created it no longer feels free to express his ideas as naturally and joyfully as he did before. It is as though he cannot compete with what he considers to be his own best self. And in many instances the creative effort of the other children is snuffed out by the demon Competition.

The poem is never the all-important thing. The deep emotional satisfactions that children gain from expressing their innermost thoughts are what really count. This is the reason we want children to become acquainted with the power of original expression that lies within all of us. We want them to know that this power is theirs and to have faith to use it. We want them to dig beneath clichés and accepted patterns of thought to find out what they really think and feel.

If we are to achieve a richer culture, rich in human potentialities, we must recognize the whole gamut of human personalities and so weave a less arbitrary social fabric, one in which each human gift will find a fitting place. — MARGARET MEADE, From the South Seas

6. Individual Differences in Writing

CASE studies of seven children, ranging in ability from average to highly gifted, present a clearer picture of growth than any amount of description can portray. Selections of their writing, both personal and practical, taken from the latter four years of the elementary school, reveal some of the basic trends of maturation and learning. From these samplings it is self-evident that each child lends his unique quality to his writing when he is allowed to do so, and that this uniqueness is effective style. The obligation to learn correct forms in practical writing and the manner in which children can and do apply these forms in personal writing are shown as each child develops. And conversely, it appears that children color their utilitarian writing with that delightful individuality fostered by their free and copious expression of imagination and invention.

Seven cases reveal the growth of seven different personalities, each over a period of four years. Could we present a hundred of those we have worked with, the result would be a hundred cases, each as different as are these seven. We have sought, therefore, to select those that give an honest cross section of the children we have studied. It is true that all these children were of average or superior ability, for we have felt it unfair to describe so personally those of inferior power because of the possibility of identification. But even weaker children showed visible growth.

Only seven of the one hundred and twenty children included in our four groups are presented. A more exact picture could, of course, be sketched if all were presented, since every child grows in his own particular way. The children were different at the beginning of our study; naturally they were more different at the end of the four years, as age always increases divergences of ability. One general statement can be made with truth concerning those who were in our groups for several years: at the end of the sixth grade each child was writing with a feeling of satisfaction and security in the undertaking, with eagerness and with courage. And we can say with equal honesty that no groups with whom we have used more conventional methods have approached the degree of control shown by these children over accepted English essentials of form, structure, and organization. It has become our sure conviction that every writing experience, lived joyfully and richly, contributes to the maximum development of writing power.

All children under nine or ten years of age are poets and philosophers. — E. DIMNET, Art of Thinking

FIRST CASE STUDY — RUTH

Ruth entered our school at third grade and came into a group notable for its *esprit de corps.* The children welcomed her warmly, but were at the same time abashed by her shyness. She was frail from recent illness and naturally a bit awkward because of being strange to a group that had known one another for at least two years. There was a kind of glow about her, however, that made her easily accepted without its being necessary for the teacher to promote friendships, as one so frequently must do for newcomers. Coupled with this friendliness was an unusual timidity, to which a number of circumstances had contributed. This diffidence limited the effectiveness of her abilities, which, though not at all outstanding, were adequate for normal growth. She needed constant assurance of her power to enter into the various activities of the group and even to cope with routine tasks.

During the first half of third grade the children continued storytelling and dictating. Though she had always been an appreciative listener, it was not until after Christmas that Ruth ventured to tell a short story. When, near the end of the year, a few of the children began to write stories, Ruth, after frequent assurances that it "would be all right," wrote the following stiff and meager tale. This reproduction of her own handwriting shows the strain under which she worked. A printed copy is included for easier reading.

Tale of a Monkey

Once upon a time in a jungle lived a monkey. He had a lot of friends. This little monkey always play tricks. One day all the little monkeys were playing under a plam tree. But one. He threw down a coconut. All the little monkeys looket up and ran away.

Even a sympathetic and hopeful teacher can find nothing promising in this story. But it was Ruth's first and was therefore important. Indeed, all first stories are important and this one especially so because of the timidity that had held the child. This feeble attempt was courteously accepted by the group. Appreciative reception, along with her delight in actually seeing her own story on paper, proved so tempting that in spite of her fear of failure Ruth was eager to try again.

Because writing had once been fun, her practical writing also began to show improvement. She now worked with zest at most of the tasks which up to this time had been burdensome. Another year of growth, continued building of self-confidence, and further experience in writing with satisfaction began to free her from her earlier fears. The following story written at nine years gives evidence of a developing ease and fluency in marked contrast to the stiffness and poverty of the "Tale of a Monkey." In her typically uncertain way Ruth asked for many corrections while writing. Hence in this corrected version only quotation marks and a few changes in spelling were needed.

When I Was A Little Girl

When I was a little girl I didn't like to go to bed. One night Mother had a dinner party. I thought I would listen to what they said. So when they went into dinner, I sneaked into the living room and hid behind the couch. I waited and waited till finally they came in. Some people sat on the couch and talked. They had long dresses on. Pretty soon they started dancing. I had never seen anything so funny in my life. Pretty soon I started laughing. Everybody got scared. I felt awfully bad and crouched down. Everybody asked where the sound came from. Someone said, "Over there." Daddy looked behind the couch and saw me. He yelled, "You bad girl, don't you do that any more." And I never did.

By reading the story with all the dramatic power she could summon, the teacher saw to it that Ruth had the satisfaction of

Individual Differences in Writing 145

an audience's spontaneous approval. Even though the story had not sufficient merit to be read again to the class, it had served its purpose in keeping alive Ruth's desire to write. At the same time the experience in telling a story had done much for Ruth's growth in fluency of expression. Obviously the first sentence sets the stage quite directly for the action of the story. Compare the use of the beginning complex sentence with the jerky beginning of "Tale of a Monkey." Note also the use of such graphic verbs as *sneaked* and *crouched,* as well as the use of conversation in an effective climax. Though this story does not campare with those written by other children in the group, either in imagination or in style, it does show for Ruth a real growth in conception of plot and suppleness of phrasing.

During the next year experience with uncriticized personal writing helped considerably in freeing Ruth's imagination. Greater control of mechanics resulting from further practical writing gave her an increased confidence. She developed some power of invention, but still needed the comfort of an adult's approval. She asked if each detail of her story "would be all right." Given needed support, she was able without further help to carry out her plan effectively.

In the sixth grade she wrote with comparative case in both the utilitarian and imaginative fields, though she occasionally asked for help that she did not really need but which gave her the assurance that she still wanted. She accepted for herself high standards of clarity in informational writing, as can be seen in the following excerpts from a comprehensive report on "Tobacco." Ruth divided her material, culled from reading and conversations with a recent visitor to Cuba, into five sections: Growing, Curing, Tobacco Uses, Statistics, and, of course, References. "This is getting much too long," she complained on the seventh page of handwriting, "but it's all part of the report and I don't see how I can leave any of it out." Only parts of each section can be included here, since the final report was four full typewritten pages.

Tobacco

Growing

Tobacco grows mostly anywhere in the earth except where it does not rain often enough for the soil to be moistened. It takes a great amount of patience to take care of tobacco from when it is first planted in a seed bed. (The farmer has to plant the tobacco in a bed first because the tiny black seeds are so small that 60,000 of them make one tablespoon, enough to sow 100 square yards of seed bed.) . . .

Curing

Curing is done when the tobacco leaves are fully grown and they are taken to a barn or put under a cheesecloth to be dried in the sun. Tobacco cured in a closed barn by means of hot air is called "flue cured." Tobacco cured in a curing shed is called "air cured." After tobacco is all cured sometimes the cured leaves are shriveled up half their size and many times one third their regular size. . . .

Tobacco Uses

Tobacco is used for five or six purposes. They are snuff, smoking, cigarettes, cigars, and chewing tobacco. . . .

SNUFF

There is a certain kind of tobacco grown for snuff. It has a very strong flavor. Snuff tobacco is ground up to a very fine powder. It is then used by people who like to sneeze. They take a pinch and place it in their nose and then sneeze. In the olden days the men used to carry the snuff under their cuffs. They had very small boxes and very elaborate ones. . . .

CIGARS

(Note: The following is a description of how cigars are made in Cuba, as described by a person who saw them made.)

There are four things that people do in a cigar factory. There are girls that wear white gloves who take the largest tobacco leaves and split them down the center vein. Then the split leaves are given to a man who does the first step in sorting the tobacco. He takes the split leaves and sorts them into about twelve different piles according to their color. This man has to have excellent eyesight. He must have the light coming from the north. There are about 100 different colors and there is a very slight difference between them. The lightest cigars are the mildest. . . .

The scope of information treated here and the detail included indicate the thoroughness of Ruth's preparation before writing. She listed questions before she started her reading of references and added to them in our conferences. These questions shaped the general organization of her paper, which seems to us admirably carried out. (Ruth wrote this when eleven years old.) The detailed background, along with the control gained by frequently talking over her ideas and findings with the whole group, enabled Ruth to write with greater power.

Of course, increased maturity also accounts in part for her use of more involved sentence structure. "After the cigars are made they are taken to a man who sorts them into piles according to their color" — a complex sentence with two dependent clauses was used naturally by a child who understood the relationships existing before she tried to verbalize them. Note also that the sentences vary in length, construction, and order. One cannot help but note the frequent bridging over from near-adult constructions to quite delightfully childlike expressions. "It is then used by people who like to sneeze" — is very immature both in form and in point of view. It suggests the amusement felt by Ruth and others of the group at what seemed to them phenomenal. Sneezing meant having a cold and having to stay in bed. Just imagine liking that! In contrast to this juvenile reaction to the use of snuff, the transitional sentences introducing the uses of tobacco are remarkable. Ruth presents a new phase of her subject and indicates five subordinate but pertinent topics in clean-cut fashion. Control of the subject matter is evident in her organization.

In the sixth grade the group was studying medieval life. Following several weeks of group study and building a common background, each child selected one phase of the study for individual pursuit. Ruth chose the daily life in the monasteries and, after general reading and discussion, made the following plan for her report: Daily Religious Life, The Rule, Work, Writing, and Clothing.

Only the first two paragraphs of her report are included here, but these are enough to indicate the increasing smoothness of phraseology and more dignified style appropriate to her subject.

Six times a day the monks gather for prayer and singing of psalms in the chapel. Again at midnight the bell called them from their hard couches to services. The monks who cultivated the field did not come to the chapel for every service but they would kneel on the ground and pray till the service was over.

The "Rule" of the monastery at all times ordered that they should "speak slowly without laughter, humbly with gravity, with few and sensible words." At meals they sat silently while one monk (who was allowed to eat earlier) read from some religious book.

Monks did more than just pray and have services all day. Each monk had his own task. Some worked in the kitchen, some in the monastery garden, some would tend to the cattle and sheep. Some gathered fuel, others tilled the fields, some cobbled shoes, others wove baskets until in a short time there came to be a thousand and one different occupations. The monks were assigned to different jobs by the head of the monastery to which they were best suited.

In spite of the misplaced clause in the final sentence of this excerpt, this is an excellent piece of paragraph construction for an eleven-year-old child. Note the transition sentence, "Monks did more than just pray and have services all day," taking the reader from the first two paragraphs about religious services to the specialized tasks each monk performed for his monastery. Note also the variety of sentence length, the repetition for emphasis, and the economy with which the concluding idea is presented. Growing confidence is evident in content, phrase, and form.

By this time Ruth thoroughly enjoyed writing and wove her own friendly sense of humor into her stories in a truly effective manner. It seems scarcely possible that the same child who wrote with obvious fear and strain the stiff, meager "Tale of a Monkey" could, less than three years later, write with keen enjoyment this gay and well-constructed story. Ruth laughed as

wholeheartedly as any of the other children over the events of
Mr. Martin's evening. Her first draft, which concludes this
study, shows, also, the growth in mechanics and co-ordination.

Cooking Difficulties

Mr. Martin I must tell you was not an expert cook. His wife
and children had been invited to a dinner party but *of course* he
wouldn't be invited. He sat perched in an easy chair with the
evening paper in his hand, cigar in his mouth and radio on. The
clock hands ran around till Mr. Martin became hungry. He strolled
out to the kitchen wondering what to eat that was different; by
this I mean besides mashed potatoes, lamb chops, and lima beans.
He hastily pulled out the cook book. Finally his eyes sighted a
picture that made his mouth water. The picture was of Devils'
Food Cake. He started putting sugar and eggs in a bowl and began
mixing them. The draft blew in from the window and the old
wind puffed at the cook book and a few pages flopped over. Mr.
Martin was too busily beating the eggs and sugar to notice the
pages turn over. As his eye glanced back to see what was next to
go in the bowl the next thing his eye saw was two cups of vinegar
so in went the vinegar, wesson oil, salt, pepper. Then he put it all
in a pan and put it in the oven. Mr. Martin turned the temperature gadget up to 520°. He then began to hear a funny noise. He
hastened over to the oven; and there right before his eyes his sup-
posedly devil's food cake was bubbling, fizzling, popling and doing
everything. Mr. Martin got thoroughly disgusted; he stamped his
foot, shut off the oven, turned off the lights. Mr. Martin then went
down town to eat dinner at a restaurant, bought a box of cigars
and went to a Mae West picture show.

What more typically human anticlimax could be imagined?
The warm and humorous appreciation of simple, homey situations is as much a part of Ruth as of her story. Her perception
of adult foibles and frustrations is both amazing and disconcert-
ing. She maneuvered Mr. Martin into a ridiculous situation
but with no cruelty in her treatment. Through graphic detail
Ruth achieved a climax in which the oven's sound effects are
exceeded only by Mr. Martin's noisy activities of retreat. Ruth
has maintained her characterization of a comfort-loving person
from the first sentence to the last.

Cooking Difficulties

Mr. Martain I must tell you was not an expert cook. His wife and children had been invited to a dinner party but of <u>course</u> he wouldn't be invited. He sat perched in an easy chair with the evening paper in his hand, cigar in his mouth and radio on. The clock hands ran around till Mr. Martin became hungry He strolled out to the kitchen wondering what to eat that was different; by this I mean besides mashed potatos, lamb chops, and lima beans. He hastily pulled out the cook book. Finally his eyes sighted a picture that made his mouth water. The picture was of Devil's Food Cake. He started putting sugar and eggs in a bowl and began mixing them. The draft blew in from the window and the old wind puffed at the cook book and a few pages flopped over. Mr. Martin was too busily beating the eggs and sugar to notice the pages turn over. As his eye glanced back to see what was next to go in the

This handwriting, contrasted with that of Ruth's first

150

bowl the next thing his eye saw was two
cups of vinegar so in went the vinegar.
Finally after putting into the bowl
sugar, eggs, vinegar, wesson oil, salt, pepper,
Then he put it all in a pan and put it
in the oven. Mr. Martin turned the oven
tempeture gadget up to 520° He then began
to hear a funny noise. He hasend
over to the oven; and there right
before his eyes his suposedly devil
food cake was bubbling, frizzling,
popling and doing every thing. Mr.
Martin got thruely disqusted he stamped
his foot, shut of the oven turned of
the lights. Mr. Martin then went
down town to eat dinner at a
restaurant, bought a box of cigars
and went to a ~~Mae West~~ picture
show.

story, gives evidence of relaxation and assurance.

*. . . yet, even like an ocean, you cannot
hasten your tides.* — KAHLIL GIBRAN, The
Prophet

SECOND CASE STUDY — DANNY

Danny was the middle child in a lively, capable household. Shy and frail, he very early built for himself a protecting cocoon of silence and docility, within which he lived an exciting life of his own devising. Out of the abundance of interests to which he was constantly exposed, he took for himself only those things that he wanted and moved along untouched by the rest. Thus with an intuitive wisdom he preserved and nurtured his unique self, although by the same process he developed an indifference to directed learning that has made his academic progress slow.

When Danny first came to school, he rarely talked. If he had to communicate with adults, he hid his face in his hands, and mumbled so thickly that his words were scarcely intelligible. Fortunately he found release in doing things. He was a busy child, cluttering up his room at home with roughly made toys or "inventions," and following at school some engrossing interest that was usually quite unlike what any other child was doing. It was not that Danny was unco-operative with children. On the contrary he displayed a friendly eagerness to help, but his vital activity — the kind that engaged his power — followed an independent course. And it was only as we examined his self-designed experiments that we began to appreciate his potential strength.

Through the early school years Danny continued to be a diffident, inarticulate child. Toward the close of the second grade, however, after he had been with the same teacher for almost two years, he felt enough confidence to dictate a few stories — some at home and others at school. One of these follows. In it he tells the story of his own craving. He is the weak and puny little rabbit that longs so passionately to be big and strong like the older ones in his family.

The Rabbit Who Liked Carrots

Once there was a little rabbit who liked carrots so much he ate them every day. One day he had some lettuce, but he wanted some carrots and he said he didn't have any for a long time. One day his mother kept on giving him more carrots and more carrots and more carrots until he got sick. When he was well again he still wanted carrots so his mother told him where he could find them because she was tired of picking them for him. So he went there and ate up all the carrots and he didn't have any more. He wondered what to do.

One day he decided to go out and hunt for some more. On he went, and on and on and on till he came to another city where everything was very big and where he came upon some carrots and the carrots were very, very big. They were as tall as trees to him. Then he saw a man coming. The man, who was a very big man, asked him what he wanted. The rabbit told him he wanted the carrots so the man took out his knife and cut the littlest piece he could, but still it was bigger than the rabbit. So the rabbit said, "Give me the littlest knife you have in the city and maybe I can cut it." So the man gave him the knife, but when the rabbit got it he could hardly lift it. So the man helped him till he got the piece he wanted. He ate on and on till he grew very big like the other rabbits in the city.

He went home, but when he got to his house, he was too big to get in. So he went where the carrots were, but the carrots seemed so little to him that he could scarcely see them. Then he heard a voice. It was a fairy. He looked around a bit till he saw the fairy, who was very hard to see because it was so tiny. The fairy said he'd have to live in her house six weeks before he'd be small again. He couldn't fit in the castle so he stayed outside. The fairy took her wand and touched a place in the ground and there grew a big castle, big enough for him to get into. So he stayed in that castle six weeks and then went home where he lived happily ever after.

Over and over again we have had from young children similar stories or rhythmic chantings that were vigorous and sincere because they had been prompted by deep-seated personal impulses and desires. However, many forces operate to close the channels through which this original self emerges. With Danny language expression was curtailed because his third year began with a new teacher. Again afraid, he slipped back into his sheltering cocoon. He followed what went on in the group as though he were an outsider, and in a detached, dutiful way did only what seemed to be required. Nothing broke through his defense until small groups began giving playlets. These he watched with obvious enjoyment. Gradually, very gradually, he began to take part. At first he was only a mover of scenery; later he performed small bits in pantomime, and, finally, by the spring of his fourth year he was doing very short speaking parts with some degree of confidence. During this time he had told no stories, although in the last months of the fourth year he wrote two short ones.

This early history scarcely prepared us for what Danny did in his fifth year. Again he had a new teacher, and again he assumed his uncommunicative role. That fall the teacher began the writing periods by reading a variety of things, some from her files of fifth- and sixth-grade work and others from adult authors. The children were invited, though not urged, to contribute anything they had written. At first the offerings were disheartening. Little came and that little was lifeless and dull. Nevertheless, the contributions were read with as much enthusiasm as the teacher could muster. One morning she chanced to give them Sterling North's "Five Little Bears and the Milkman." The next day Danny handed in a tale of his own about the same characters. Eyes lighted up as the teacher read the new version, and there was a clamor to know who had written it. The hearty approval his story received worked a magical change in Danny. From that moment he began to grow visibly in poise and power. Although writing cost him great effort, every few days he produced a new story for our enjoyment. At length he persuaded his father to be his scribe, and the stories laboriously written at school were supplemented by those dictated at home. Experiences of the Five Bears were continued, and other series were invented. For many readings Danny held the class enthralled by the adventures of the great Chimino, the second chapter of which follows. Even at this early stage he had learned, when ending one chapter, how to whet the appetite for the next. In this story and the one following, appropriate changes in mechanics have been made to facilitate reading.

The Adventures of Chimino, Chapter II

It was not long before Chimino met his first adventure. He came to the edge of a canyon completely made of glass. The sides were smooth so that he could not climb down and at the bottom there was a fiery dragon.

Chimino scratched his head and wondered how he could climb down. Finally he had an idea. He took one of his pills and then he let himself over the side of the canyon slowly. Then he kicked the glass with his foot and made a foothold. He did this several times until he finally came to the bottom. Then he traveled the best he could on the glass, but often slipped. Before long a fierce growl met him. He looked up and there was a fiery dragon.

Chimino took out his sword and hit the dragon with it. The dragon was very angry at this so at once he jumped around, but slid on the glass and fell flat on his back. Then Chimino jumped on him, but the dragon jumped up and kicked Chimino. Before long it was a regular mix-up. Chimino and the dragon were slipping all around the canyon. The dragon shot fire on one side while Chimino sprang around to the other. Then the dragon would quickly jump around, while Chimino sprang over to the other side and the dragon slipped on his back. Then Chimino jumped on him and lashed him with his sword.

Before long Chimino won and at once continued his travels. In a short time he came to the other side. He climbed up in the same manner in which he had climbed down, although he slipped a few times and nearly lost his life.

When he got to the top he came to the same kind of forest that he did at first. Finally he got through to the other side, where he saw the wildest land he had ever seen in his life. It was all swamp and mushy, and there were a few trees that were very high and bigger than ordinary. All across the sky were black blotches. One seemed to get bigger and bigger. Suddenly an enormous black

monster blotted out the whole sun. His huge hand quickly grasped
Chimino and carried him away.

Although the Chimino stories gave full scope for Danny's
love of invention, his bear stories were more revealing. The
one that follows has an imagined setting — the old-fashioned
school with the dunce cap, the answer book, the whippings —
but it is peopled with characters from his own environment:
the absent-minded teacher, the boy who hid the chalk, the fair-
minded, energetic mother, and even Danny himself. In the
character of Mo he exposes his own reactions to life — his ex-
perimental attitude, his childlike way of reasoning, his im-
munity to punishment, and his open delight in getting ahead
of adults.

It was Mo's second day at school. He had lately tried out some
experiments, and he had found out that if you pushed pencils off
people's desks, they got sent down to the principal to be whipped.
And also he had found out that there was no school on Saturday
or Sunday.

Now it happened that Mo was in school or rather in the dunce
chair admiring the dunce hat that he was wearing. He had just
lately tried to get out of school another way. Then he said to
himself, "What good is it to get Roy sent down to the principal if
I don't see him whipped?"

So while he was waiting he grabbed the chalk that the teacher
had put down on the desk when she wasn't looking. The teacher,
without noticing this action, got another piece of chalk. Then she
said,

"Roy Bear, what is three times two times six times eight?"

"It's the same as eight times six times two times three," Roy
answered.

"That's no answer," said the teacher.

"It's fifty-four," whispered Meinie into Roy Bear's ear.

The teacher gave Meinie a severe look. "What's the answer, Roy
Bear?" repeated the teacher.

"Fifty-four," said Roy Bear.

"Wrong," said the teacher.

"Then what is the answer?" said Roy Bear.

"I don't know," said the teacher. "I'll have to look it up in my
answer book."

By this time Mo had taken a full box of chalk from the teacher, and the teacher was looking in the cupboard for another one. So Mo grabbed the pointer and hit Roy Bear over the head with it.

"Ow-w-w!" yelled Roy Bear.

The teacher jumped ten feet in the air. She was so startled.

"What do you mean by making such a noise?" she asked. "You ought to be whipped. In fact you will be. Go down to the principal at once."

So Roy Bear walked out of the room. While Eenie was giggling to himself, Mo calmly took off his dunce cap, put it on a chair, and then walked toward the door.

"Where are you going, Mo?" asked the teacher.

"To see Roy Bear whipped," said Mo.

"Why do you want to see Roy Bear whipped?" asked the teacher.

"Because I banged him over the head so he would yell and get whipped. So it is only fair that I should see it."

"There is something in what you say," said the teacher, "but I was the one that sent him down, and so I should go down and see him get whipped too."

"The only one who has seen him get whipped so far is the principal," said Mo.

"Then I shall go down and watch him get whipped and I think that I will fire the principal and take her place."

"I don't think I need you along," said Mo quickly.

"Oh, yes you do," said the teacher. "Come here."

"Goodbye," said Mo. "Hope you have a nice time," and he ran out slamming the door in the teacher's face.

Now the principal didn't have as much pleasure as the teacher thought she did for the principal was blind. Mo was running down the hall with the teacher right at his heels. He could hear the yowls and shrieks of Roy Bear, but this was not unusual because he heard them every day. The principal was just reaching out for Roy Bear, but Roy ducked and she accidentally grabbed the teacher and began whipping her. Roy Bear and Mo laughed and laughed. Then Mo climbed out the window and ran all the way home and said to Mother Bear in an excited voice:

"Do you know what I did, Mother? I banged Roy Bear over the head so he got sent down to the principal and by mistake the principal whipped our teacher. And oh, it was funny," he said, wiping a tear out of his eye. "And do you know what Eenie did? He told Roy Bear the wrong answer to a problem and Roy Bear got heck."

"Oh, he did, did he?" said Mother Bear who was very angry. So she put on her coat and went all the way down to school. When she got there, she saw the teacher crawling back to her room. So she helped the teacher up, and then she went in and pulled the other four bears out by their ears. She took them home and put them to bed with Mo.

In bed Nig said to Mo, "Gosh, Mo, what did you squeal for? You always are a big tattletale."

"Oh, I couldn't help it," said Mo. "I was just telling Mother Bear how funny you were," and he began to laugh.

So Nig tried to go to sleep, while Eenie and Meenie played rock, stone, and paper, and Meinie tried to figure out what three times six times two times eight was.

The heart-warming success of his bear stories seemed to vanquish Danny's fears. From the day he read the first one, he gained confidence steadily and soon became an energizing influence in the class. Longer than most children he had stayed on in the inquisitive, seeking stage. He felt a naive and serious wonder in everything he did, so that learning retained for him the fresh excitement of personal discovery. Whatever ideas he chose to consider were not passive abstractions to be stored away or verbally rehearsed; they were dynamic suggestions to be tried out at once. When he saw his brother enlarging a map at home, he found out how it was done. The next morning he came to school early, asked for a big piece of paper, and set to work on the floor making a large map of Greece, the country we were then studying. When the opportunity came to work on the auditorium lighting, he not only learned how to manipulate the switches, but he equipped his home puppet stage with as elaborate a system as he could manage. When the family got a new automobile, Danny, who so short a while before had side-stepped all speaking in public, begged for a chance to talk to the group. He told in detail how a gasoline engine works, and later came to school with an excellent illustrative model made from tin cans. These are but a few of the interests that his active curiosity followed, and with which he infected others in the group. His quiet but wholehearted enthusiasm spread a contagion that few of the boys could resist.

Because Danny put so much feeling and tireless effort **into** his work, one would naturally expect his craftsmanship to be of superior quality, but that was not the case. Apparently he was so stirred by doing and discovering that he failed to see his results apart from his dreams. As a consequence he exhibited with proud satisfaction work that to us was distressingly crude and untidy. The glaring defects were not due to lack of interest or exertion; they were the reflection of Danny's immaturity. Until he had developed more manual skill and had gained the power to view his work more objectively, overemphasis on points of correctness could only confuse him. Therefore, in practical mechanics, we held him to as high standards as we thought he could reasonably accomplish, and we did not urge him beyond those. We believed that if we could preserve that deep personal concern in what he did, he would master the necessary skills when he came to see the need and had acquired sufficient muscular control.

Undoubtedly the fifth grade was the turning point in Danny's school history, for it was then that he broke free from the fears that had restrained him. The early years of stubborn struggle had strengthened his courage, but the success of his storytelling gave the needed spur. During the sixth grade, he continued to develop along the lines already begun. So it is that whenever we think of Danny, our faith in the force of personal expression is renewed. To remember him literally sweating over his smudgy papers tells us how important creative effort was to him. To realize the change that was worked in Danny himself reveals how potent such effort can be in establishing self-faith and in releasing pent-up power.

No bird soars too high if he soars with his own wings. — W. BLAKE, Poems and Prophecies

THIRD CASE STUDY — JOANNE

On the playground Joanne was such a rough and tumble little harum-scarum that one would scarcely suspect the sensitive, fanciful nature her writing revealed. In the classroom she was the teacher's delight — and her despair. Her poetic imagination, her humor, her feeling for the dramatic, and her eager aliveness gave color and joy to the school day; but her spelling, her arithmetic, her penmanship, and her housekeeping refused to conform to accepted standards. Her whole nature intuitively resisted set pattern and routine. Even though she well knew that six times two are twelve, she disliked having it be that *every* time. She could invent freely, abundantly, joyously; but she could not imitate. Copying was almost impossible for her to do correctly, and even a finished picture bore little resemblance to her initial sketch. Attempts to direct her creative work were fruitless. She promptly lost interest in the thing discussed and turned to something else. In this simple, effective way she maintained her creative integrity.

In the third-year group Joanne was the first to express herself poetically, and from the beginning her individual expression was fresh and rhythmical and strong. The fun she had in voicing her ideas was so genuine that the desire to do likewise quickly infected others. Her childish ponderings were transmuted into lyrics. "Me," dictated late in that third year, expressed in its rhythmic pattern, as clearly as in its words, the inadequacy a little girl can feel.

Me

When my mother plays on the piano
Her fingers dance like fairies
In the summer on the grass
Or like fireflies dancing at night.
But when I try to play
I put my fingers down on the keys
And the piano goes
Thump, bang, thump, ping.
It's like a giant stamping all over the land.

"Paper White Narcissus," dictated a year later, tells that there are fairy children, too, who cannot remember the practical and the mundane.

Paper White Narcissus

You know that flower called Paper White Narcissus?
Well, the fairies use it for paper
To write their letters on,
And for their children who can't remember
What they have to get from the store —
A dozen ant eggs, or a pound of dandelion leaves,
That's what Paper White Narcissus are used for.

In the fifth year there was for Joanne, as well as for the rest of the group, a decided dropping off in poetical expression. The teacher, though sympathetic, was new, and so there was a slight constraint. There was more drive on academic work, and less opportunity for the teacher to be the scribe for the children's ideas. Perhaps, too, there were changes in the children themselves that led to different kinds of expression. The compact lyrical form may be more natural to the younger age. We do not know. Whatever the reason, Joanne turned to stories and to playing with the sounds of words. Often a tempting title was made up first, such as "Why Witches Are Waterproof," or "The Short, Short Sink That Went to Heaven," and then a fitting story concocted. She struggled earnestly to be her own amanuensis, with results that were untidy, inaccurate, and often half-finished. Her clerical power could not keep pace with her flashing mind. But even under such difficulties she continued to experiment, to find joy in the doing, and to produce a few things that were truly good. Sometimes sound and rhythm engrossed her, quite to the exclusion of sense. In "The Haunted House" there are music and mood, but there is little logical meaning. Note in the copy the indicated improvement she made in the last line, and the directions she gave for the reading.

The Haunted House

Once there was a house on the grey still ground;
Once there was a house all misty with fog.
Once there was a house and ghosts lived in it.
Once there was a house all boards a-shaking.
Once there was a house. Nine grey old men lived in it.
(Fast, lightly) Down by the wayside there's that house.
(Slowly) Witches are in it, but DON'T go there.

The Hanted house
By

Once there Was
a house on the
grey still grounds.
Once there was a
house, all misTy
with fog. Once there
was a house and
and gosts lived
in it. ~~and~~ ~~plab~~
~~or a spirt~~

Once There was a
house all boards
a slaking. Once more
a house niha grey
Old men Was men lived fast lightley
in it. ~~Done~~ ~~De~~ Down By
the Way Side theres
that house. slowley Witohs are
in it, but Don't! go
there.
The End

Joanne's original work sheet shows her experimentation with rhythm.

162

Everything that Joanne did consistently revealed the free, intuitive worker that she was. Her arithmetic, after the first few examples, never went in orderly rows, and her writing jumped from pigmy to giant in a single line. Her art work was distinguished by its spontaneity and its rhythmic movment, and even her factual reports were transformed by her imagination into episodes that were vivid and alive. During her fifth year she made a study of ants, at the end of which she submitted the following resumé. It is not a report at all, but a fanciful incident focused dramatically on the queen and the royal eggs. In it, however, an abundance of information is evident, information that she has made truly her own. Since it was to be part of a class book, Joanne, with her teacher, edited her report to this extent.

My Trip Through The Ant Hill

"Oh, Mr. Guide," I said, "what is that tunnel and why is it so long?" "Well," said the guide, "it's this way. The queen of this state is laying eggs there and does not want to be disturbed." "Do you think she would mind me seeing her?" I said. "Well, I'll see," said the guide; so he went to the door. "Knock, knock." "Yes," came a voice. "What do you want?" "Well," said the guide, "I have a visitor and she wants to see you." "Show her in," said the voice again. The guide led me through many passages till he came to a door. "Knock, knock." "Come in. I am expecting you." The guide opened the door and bowed. "Your — your — Majesty," blushed the guide, "here is your visitor." I had seen many things, but none so beautifully made. The walls were solid and hard and shining dirt. All were even with no faults anywhere. After awhile the queen said, "Do you know how I make my kingdom?" and she laughed, "I should say queendom. Well," she went on, "I lay eggs and every once in a while I lay a royal egg which is a male or prince or queen. The male and queen are rare; but prices quite common." "Oh," I said, "that's interesting. I always thought . . . Well I don't know what I thought." "Well," she said, "you had better be going because I have to lay my eggs." The guide took me out and said, "Would you like to see our workers? You know," he said as he went along, "we only have a few men and women to mate. Most of our people are workers which are neither males or females." "Oh," I said, "that seems impossible." "Well, it isn't," he said.

By this time we had reached a tunnel. An ant was guarding it.
"No one allowed!" he said excitedly. "No one allowed! Danger of
falling pebbles. No one allowed. It is a newly made tunnel and
we are making room for the royal eggs. No one allowed!" And I
saw a pile of white eggs or cocoons. I looked closely and a black
head peeked out of one. Then came the body. Then we went on.
Suddenly a great commotion fell over the ant hill. All subjects were
running to and fro. The new tunnel was finished and eggs were
being stored away. I asked my guide what was happening and he
said, "There is a war and we are against the red ants. Most of our
workers are fighting and not many are left to do the storing of
eggs." Soon the war was over and it was victory for the Black Ants.
"Well I must be going now," I said. And that ends my chapter and
I hope you enjoyed it.

The End

This is not a true story.

That same spring, caught up in the class enthusiasm for "The
Five Bears," Joanne wrote a story strongly marked by her individual traits. It has little plot, but is rather a series of lively
pictures with touches of fun and with shrewd observations of
human behavior.

The Five Bears Have a Spring Festival
With Surprising Results

PART I

"Ma!" called Mo as he came down the path, "we're having a
Spring what-cha-ma-call-it, and I dress up as the Big Bad Wolf.
Eenie, Meenie, and Meinie are the three pigs and Nig's the announcer. Sue's the Mother Pig. She has to fasten two pillows in
front of her to make her fat and some string on for a tail, and you,"
he added, crossing his arms, "have to make us jackets."

"Well," said Mrs. Bear for the first time that she was able to
speak, "well, that's nice."

"Ma! Ma! got to tell you sumpin'," yelled Meenie, dashing down
the path with the other three bears at his heels.

Then Mo said calmly, "I told it all."

"Oh!" Meenie's jaw dropped, "you would."

"No, he didn't," said Mother, "what is it?"

"Well," Meenie brightened up, "it's a festival — a spring festival. Nice?"

PART II

The time had come. All the mother bears were chattering in the classroom, sitting in the children's chairs. Now and then a bear's face would peek out, or rather a pig's face or Red Riding Hood. Then Nig stepped out.

"Ladies and perfume bottles," said Nig — he was so confused by the smell of perfume. "We are having a May — rather a fest — oh! no, no, we're having a play."

He disappeared through the curtains amid the titters and giggles of the mothers. The curtains opened with a jerk .

"Hey, it's not ready," said a voice, and then the curtains closed again. This statement was greeted by a roar of laughter.

Five minutes later the curtains opened again. This time Eenie was sitting by a paper hut. He began to sing, "I build my house of horsehair — I mean hay. I build my house of hay, hay, hay. Oh, here comes Mo — I mean the wolf," he said as he ran off the stage.

The wolf paused only to push the house down and then he ran off. All went well until the wolf was supposed to come down the chimney. The pot had a pillow in it so as not to hurt Mo, but just then Eenie yelled, "The pot's not there!" But it was too late. The wolf had fallen and that started a fight. The curtain closed on the unpleasant scene. The class acted a play, *Red Riding Hood,* but the bears did not see it for the night found all five bears tenderly rubbing their seats in bed.

Although Joanne reveals originality and distinction in her writing, she has been woefully inadequate in the skills. Through the fifth grade she had evaded all our efforts to teach her as persistently as a boy escapes washing the back of his neck — and for the same reasons. In her eyes, to spell and write correctly were hard work and were useless. She was having fun playing with her mind, and she wasn't caring at all about appearances. Of course, we could have been insistent and perhaps thereby have made Joanne a better speller, but we might have stopped all spontaneous outpouring. So, instead, we lowered the usual demands made in practical writing to match her undeveloped power, and we watched to commend her slightest effort to improve her use of the prescribed skills. Now in her sixth school year our faith and forbearance are being justified. Joanne was eleven when suddenly she came to care about her use of tool techniques, and she exerted enough well-directed effort to accomplish reasonable mastery of them. Probably she will always find it difficult to conform to set patterns, to discipline that pixie spirit within her. But she will, we are now convinced, manage to write with acceptable correctness and, we hope, with unabated satisfaction and joy.

With the exercise of self-trust new powers shall appear. — EMERSON, Essays

FOURTH CASE STUDY — ARTHUR

Because Arthur appeared to be always sweet-tempered and at ease, few people realized how much he was haunted by the fear of being inadequate. Lacking all inner assurance of power, he leaned heavily on the approval of others and worked as earnestly as he knew how to deserve that approval. On the playground his athletic ability combined with his strong desire to keep everybody happy made him a popular leader, but in the classroom satisfaction did not come so easily. In his eagerness to do the expected thing he seized upon the forms, rather than the substance, of learning. Whatever the task, he set at it quickly and worked with dogged determination, though usually to the wrong purpose. In reading he aimed to call words and cover ground, in arithmetic to keep farthest ahead in assignments, and in writing to produce numbers of correct papers limited in vocabulary to his own scant spelling power. His workmanship was tidy and he was always among the first to finish because neatness and speed were to him evidences of success.

For a long time we believed he could do no better. We respected his gallant though misdirected effort and accepted gratefully such meager accounts as the following:

An Experience

One time my Mother and brother and I was walking by a lake in California and I thought I saw a fish but it was a crab. I jumped in and I nearly drowned, but my brother got a stick and pulled me out.

Then one day when the class enthusiasm for telling "poetry ideas" ran high, Arthur's feeling was so stirred that it broke through the mask that had effectually concealed him. This time he had a real experience to tell, one that had touched him intimately. Without fear or hesitation he dictated:

Orchestra

When I blow the bugle
It's such a funny noise
And when I blow it for my father
He laughs at me.
And then when I grew up
I was in a big orchestra
And my father came to watch me
And he DIDN'T laugh.

This and other dictations that followed exposed a sensitive, proud little boy who wanted too much to please people — not the dull, unimaginative child we had thought him to be.

Arthur began the next year by writing an impressive number of letters to all of the friends he had made at camp — the counsellors and caretakers as well as the boys. The following immature note is a fair sample of them all:

DEAR ROBERT DIXON:

I hope you are not sick. And I hope you are feeling well because I am. Please write soon and tell me what grade you are in. I am in the fifth grade. I guess you are in fourth grade.

Love from

ARTHUR

This was the only kind of voluntary writing he did for weeks and weeks. Eventually, however, he too began having such fun over the adventures of "The Five Bears," that again he forgot himself and made up a story called "The Pond," which surprised us by its length as well as its merit. It is strongly reminiscent of his happy life at camp, but his memories of the woods, the pond, and the games in the water have been converted by his imagination into a new story. In it he reveals a power to handle language that we had never suspected. Note the effectiveness of the opening sentence, the suggestion of character, the movement, the action, and the graphic quality of the whole. Some errors in form have been corrected for easier reading in this publication.

The Pond

On the steps of a shack on the edge of the woods were the five little bears. Their names were Eenie, Meenie, Meinie, Mo, and Nig. Meenie said, "Let's go swimming at the pond."

Mo said, "Where it is?"

Eenie said, "Don't you remember? It is about a half a mile away."

"Come on," said Meenie.

"Let's go. What are we waiting for?" said Mo. So they started down the woods without telling their mother or anyone.

Meenie said, "Don't you think we better tell Father or Mother?"

"No," said Nig, who was very bad. "Why do Mother and Father Bear always have to know where we go?"

"Oh, well, let's go," said Mo, so off they went. Soon they came to the pond.

"Here it is," said Nig, "I will beat you in."

"Oh, yeah," said Meenie.

"You wait and see," said Nig. Off went Nig's pants and shirt and off went Meenie's dress and bonnet and there was a splash and then another.

"I beat you," said Meenie.

"So what?" said Nig. And then came three more splashes.

"Let's play tag," said Eenie.

"No," said Meenie, "let's play leap frog."

"O.K.," said the rest of the bears. The pond was four feet deep.

"I am scared," said Mo, "I want to be the first one because it is too deep in the middle."

"I am not ascared," said Nig. "I will be the last one to be jumped over. Eenie, you be second. And Meenie, you be third; Meinie, you be fourth. And I will be last. Mo, you jump over Eenie and then over Meenie and then over Meinie. Last of all jump over me."

Over the first he went, then the second, then the third, and then the fourth, but where was Nig? Then they saw a lot of bubbles forming on top of the pond.

Mo said, "I bet he has drowned. How will we get him?"

"Eenie, you can swim under water. You get him," said Meinie. So under he went and brought Nig up.

"My, he looks fat," said Mo.

" He isn't fat," said Meinie.

"He drank a lot of water and he got blown up and can't talk," said Eenie.

"Let's sit up in the tree and put him under it to dry," said Meinie. So they did and while they were up there Eenie fell and landed right on Nig's stomach and all the water squirted out and he woke up.

"What happened?" said Nig.

"You blew up," said Meenie.

"WHAT?" said Nig.

"You blew up," said Mo.

"Let's go home," said Meinie.

The End

Obviously Arthur was so lacking in self-faith that he dared not reach down into himself to discover and express his own thoughts and feelings. Therefore he fed his hunger for satisfaction with the social approvals he received. All of his work was necessarily shallow and stereotyped. Only on those few occasions when a wave of feeling swept him out of his usual narrow channel of behavior did he reveal his potential power.

This case was especially meaningful to us because it indicated that we frequently may underestimate children's abilities. The customary school procedures seem to freeze them in the limiting patterns that they have already established. Undoubtedly, we need more types of learning experiences that are not set in conventional molds and in which they feel a genuine personal interest. Only through such experiences can children so free themselves that they begin to express their own possibilities.

Now it appears to me that almost any Man may, like the spider, spin from his own inwards his own Citadel — the points of leaves and twigs on which the spider begins her work are few, and she fills the air with a beautiful circuiting. — JOHN KEATS, Letters of John Keats to His Family and Friends

FIFTH CASE STUDY — LUCY

It is often surprising to see how clearly a child reveals himself in writing. An adult might have known Lucy for some time without being aware of her unique qualities. She was an unobtrusive child, sensitive and shy without being aloof, and capable with none of the aggressive or irritating characteristics that that word frequently implies. But no one could have read what Lucy wrote and remained ignorant of the nature of her personality. Even her earliest stories exposed a power of sustained logical thinking, a love of fun, a rich, but realistic imagination, and an ability to lose herself in what that imagination created. Probably the fact that she was an only child kept at home frequently by slight illnesses fostered the development of these traits. Warmhearted and lonely, she found companionship in stories — usually stories she read, but sometimes those she invented. When she was working upon one of her own, she lingered over the fun of making it up, savoring each personality, each bit of adventure, each possibility for laughter. She never created rapidly in spontaneous outbursts. Stories did not pour forth from her as they did from Joanne or Danny. Instead, they were fashioned with leisurely and affectionate care. The ideas emerged slowly and lay for some time in her mind taking on shape and depth and color. Eventually she wrote them down.

There was no need for haste because the story had been completely possessed and patterned before the writing began. Consequently her first drafts were reasonably correct and tidy. Even so they were still work sheets to Lucy and she went over them thoughtfully, substituting a more exact word here or adding there an enriching detail. Such capacity for long-continued and painstaking effort is not usual for a child. It was, however, an essential feature of Lucy's personality and was evident in all that she did. Once in clay modeling she had worked for several successive periods on the figure of a dwarf. To the teacher it looked finished and so it was set on the shelf to dry, where Lucy found it, next art period. "Oh," she demurred, "I wasn't through. There were some little things I wanted to do to it." Thus she followed her own deliberate rhythm of working toward the high standards that she herself had set.

In the second grade Lucy wrote "The Story of a Car." It is long as second-grade stories go, and it shows thoughtful planning. Moreover, in spite of all the magical happenings, it is at heart a realistic story. Upon getting its wings the car does not go adventuring in the air, as a more fanciful child might have had it do, but instead it lands *plunk!* in its own garage.

The Story of a Car

Once there was a doctor and he had a very nice car. One day the doctor had to see a sick person so he jumped into the car and off he went. While he was inside the car drove off. It went on and on. While the car was going down the road it met a kangaroo. The car stopped and asked the kangaroo to give him a pair of his hind legs. So he gave him a pair and the car went hopping off. Pretty soon it met a leopard. The car asked the leopard if he would give him some spots and he said *Yes*. So the car said *Thank you* and went on. Pretty soon he met a bird. He asked the bird to give a pair of wings. The bird said he would so the car tried to fly but the car was too heavy that the wings could not hold it up. So down the car came and *plunk* it was in its own garage.

All of Lucy's free writing has been narrative. During the next two years, when most of the children in her group were

172 *Individual Differences in Writing*

interested in reporting their "poetry thoughts," she made no contribution. Finally, toward the close of the fourth grade, she wrote "Indians," which was clearly an outgrowth of her reading. The idea, the phrases, perhaps even the design were unconsciously borrowed, but the power to imagine vividly was Lucy's own. In the picture of Fleetfoot battling the storm she succeeded in transferring her rich imagery to paper, but it was beyond her ability to continue writing in such full detail. The story grows increasingly sketchy until the climax is reduced to "a sigh of relief."

Indians

A cloud of silvery dust rose up behind the black hoofs of Fleetfoot now tan with dust. As the mare battled her way through a sand storm her black mane was sprinkled with sand. Her black coat was tan with sand. Her head low, Fleetfoot faced the storm. Her rider, Don Barton, would occasionally put his head close to Fleetfoot's ear and whisper, "We have got to warn the settlers. Indians, hear me, Fleetfoot, Indians." Don ducked as an arrow grazed his head. Another hour of hard riding and through the sand storm Don saw a ranch. At the gate Don leaped from the saddle, "Indians," he shouted. In the saddle Don warned the neighboring ranches of the attack. At the last ranch Don stopped to rest and then to fight with the rest of the men. In an hour many guns were being cleaned and bullets found. Soon an army of arrows fell upon them. Men went flying to their posts while women and children huddled together. After two hours of fighting a sigh of relief ran through the settlers. The red men had been defeated, a victory for the white men.

Less than a year later Lucy wrote "The Five Bears and William Whiskers," which shows a remarkable gain in the patience and the power necessary to record the complete story as she saw and felt it in her mind. In it there is a warm human quality and a sense of completeness that could come only with slow ripening. This was her single offering during the time that Danny produced thirty or more. While his active mind was bent on creating adventure after adventure for rather puppetlike characters,

Lucy was cultivating such an intimacy with the people about whom she wrote that what happened grew naturally out of the kind of folks they were. Undoubtedly it was Danny's unflagging and sometimes strange invention that did most to maintain the lively interest in the story-reading period during the fifth year, but it was Lucy's single story that sharpened the group's awareness for the more subtle qualities of characterization and style. A few corrections in punctuation have been added.

The Five Little Bears and
William Whiskers

One sunny afternoon the five little bears were walking the ridge pole of their roof. Their cousin, Nellie Bear, had come over to visit them. She was such a golden brown little bear that even baby Mo admired her. Nig just loved to show Nellie how far he could walk on the ridge pole without tottering too much. He was just doing that now. His arms were wide apart and the leg he wasn't standing on was always swinging. The other five bears were sitting on chimneys swinging their short fluffy legs. But Nellie didn't look very happy. She kept glancing down at the ground and holding the edge of the chimney so tight that her knuckles showed white. Just than Mo said in his small voice:

"I'm hungry," and he began to whimper.

"Oh, all right," answered Nig. "We can take some fruit home from William Whiskers, the old billy goat gardener. He won't mind."

"You hope," put in Eenie.

"Let's go down the drainpipe," said Nig.

"OK.," said Eenie. So the six little bears whizzed down the drainpipe. Splash!

"Oh, dear," said Nellie. All six little bears had landed in the rain barrel. "Oh, dear," said Nellie again, "I'm wet."

"I think," said Eenie, who was always making wise cracks, "I think we slid down the wrong drainpipe."

"I wouldn't doubt it," said Meinie.

"Well," said Nig, "let's go to the orchard. We're men. We won't let a little water stop us, will we?"

"No," said Eenie, Meenie, Meinie, and Nellie together.

"No," said Mo last of all in his weak little voice.

So they all started out for the orchard single file, Mo taking up the rear as usual. They got to the orchard, but just as they were coming out with the fruit, down the path came old William Whiskers whistling a sailor tune. He had been a sailor a long time ago, and he had beautiful red and blue tattoos up and down his arms. The little bears dashed down the path past him and into the road still holding the apples and pears. William Whiskers stopped short and then ran after them, calling, "Ahoy, there — Ahoy, there! To the starboard! Port! Drop the anchor! Blast ye!"

"There's Father's car," yelled Nig. "Jump in!"

They did. Then Nig stepped on the starter. He thought he could drive, but five minutes' driving brought them to the brink of a lake. Plunk! The car was in it. Luckily it was an open car, and in a minute up popped Nig sitting on a cushion, and last of all Nellie and Mo clinging to each other.

"What do we do now?" said Eenie, blowing the water out of his nose.

"Nothing but wait," said Nig, hitting the side of his head to get the water out of his ears.

All of a sudden apples and pears began to pop up on every side.

"They look very nice in the water, don't they?" said Meinie.

"They'd look better in my stomach," said Mo.

"I could get them if I had my butterfly net," said Meenie. You see he was very interested in insects.

"My stomach doesn't feel good," said Nellie. "Boating never did agree with it."

"Mine doesn't feel top hole either," broke in Mo weakly.

Just then William Whiskers appeared. He began to laugh. He laughed and he laughed and he laughed.

"Oh, please get us out," said Nellie.

"On one condition," said William Whiskers.

"What is it?" said Nig.

"It is," said William Whiskers, "that you stay out of my orchard."

"We will," said Mo.

"Oh, sure we will," said the rest of the little bears. Then William Whiskers got a rope and threw it out to the bears. Then he put the other end around his horns and pulled. Soon they were on the bank of the lake.

"Oh, what a relief," said Nellie, with a deep sigh.

"And we promise we won't take any more fruit," said Nig.

Everybody was happy, especially William Whiskers. But one week after if you had looked at the spikes on top of the orchard gate, you would have seen little pieces of brown fur and little pieces of blue trousers that can come off nothing but little bears.

When Lucy had finished reading "William Whiskers," the response of the class was unique. Instead of the restless, excited approval that usually greeted the stories they liked, there was a slow, deep exhalation and a fervent, "Oh, that was good!" We talked a little then — a very little — about how clearly we had seen the funny, moving pictures. We spoke, too, of how the ending had pleased us because it was exactly what might be expected of those mischievous little bears. Besides, it tempted us to go on imagining what happened the next time they got caught.

This experience illustrates how we did most of our teaching of story writing. Lessons were never worked out in advance. Instead, we seized upon an effective use of a technique when it appeared. Then by appreciation — not by precept — we focused attention upon it, hoping thereby to infect the children with its worth. This does not mean that after the single instance of talking over "William Whiskers" the next crop of stories all had excellent endings and a wealth of concrete detail. Well-rooted growth comes slowly; hence we neither expected nor desired such miracles. Our purpose was, through repeated exposure, to lead the children to recognize and to appreciate some of the factors of good writing. We knew that each child would gradually appropriate those techniques for which he was ready and use them in ways that were sincere. In the early stages we chose basic things in story structure, such as the kind of beginning that made us quickly curious, the interesting invention or surprise turning, the sense of movement, and the satisfying close. Later we watched for those more mature techniques that make for lucid and convincing style. Natural audience reactions fortified our praise. In fact we believe that it was the audience situation — the age-old situation of giving one's story directly to eager listeners — that inevitably drew forth those qualities that grip and stir the imagination. Each child, being listener and writer in turn, became increasingly aware of what to do to hold his hearers in expectant attention to the end. It was out of their successes that story form inevitably grew.

In the sixth grade Lucy wrote much more freely and abundantly. Her stories, though perhaps not so compactly organized as the one about William Whiskers, grew richer in human insight and significant detail, as is evidenced by the following excerpt from "The Hero." Through them all, too, ran an undercurrent of fun, as though she herself were highly amused by the way her characters behaved. Only two errors in form appeared in the original.

The Hero

Nig was on his bed pulling his shoes on and thinking very hard. "Gosh," he whispered, "I wonder what she's like. Maybe she's like Nellie's baby calf, but gee, I don't think I'd like that," he added, "or maybe like the puppies Roland Bear's dog had." Nig was thinking like this because his very own mother had had a baby. It was a girl. All he knew was that the five bears had to be very quiet, and he was very curious. Nig could hear Father Bear tiptoeing up the stairs. Father was trying to keep house. He pushed open Nig's door softly.

"Come down to breakfast," he hissed, and tiptoed out again.

Nig slid off the bed and followed the other bears downstairs. They had named the baby Daisy Mae. Father was doing the cooking. He had on a big checked apron and his hands were dripping with something. "Oh, can't someone help me?" he whispered almost in tears. "This is killing me. I hope we don't have any more children. Isn't six children enough?"

"I'll help," said Nig weakly. He brought in the food. The five bears grunted softly. Father Bear did not know how to cook.

"I don't think we're so hungry," hissed Mo.

Nig walked to school with half the school around him. "And," he continued, "I'm going to see her this afternoon."

"Gosh," said Roy Bear, "do you think she's real?"

"Well," answered Nig doubtfully, "I'm not so sure."

Nig was the center of attention at school. No one had ever had a baby sister before. Even the teacher was interested although Nig couldn't keep his mind on his work. "How's your mother?" she asked.

"O.K.," answered Nig. He was dreaming of little babies with wings on their backs.

The five bears were standing outside Mother Bear's door. They were all very nervous although they tried not to show it. Nig was thinking, "What if she's awful funny looking after all I've **told** the kids at school."

"I'm not so sure I want to see her," hissed Mo.

"Oh, don't be so dumb!" whispered Nig, whose knees felt **like** water. Then the door opened. Nig said, "Hello," to his mother hastily, looking the other way at a crib in a dim corner of the room. He walked over to it and peeked in. There was the sweetest little brown ball that Nig had ever seen. "Oh gee — gosh — oh my," he whispered. He was overcome with surprise. The other bears were watching the baby too. "Gee, could I touch her?" Nig asked. Mother Bear nodded. Hesitatingly Nig touched the soft little paw. He smiled down at the baby. The baby smiled back. Nig just stood there a while looking at the baby. Then he began to recover himself. He thought he must look very silly. Before he hadn't cared. Now he did. He saw Mother Bear smiling at him. "Pretty nice brat," he said, hastily trying to break the silence.

"I think she likes you best," Mother Bear answered. "She's smiling at you." Mother Bear tried to keep the amusement out of her voice. Nig blushed a deep red. Mother Bear could see his ears turning red.

"I think she's swell," cooed Mo. "Don't you, Meinie?"

"Uh huh," answered Meinie, turning pink. He knew he was in bad with Nig for saying it.

"I agree," chorused the other two bears. They were a little scared too.

After they had gone outside Nig called a conference. "Now listen," he growled in his toughest voice, "I don't think I like her so much, but I'm older and I'm more careful so when she gets old enough and can go out I'm going to take her out, see! And understand first I don't like her. I just want to take her out."

Eenie murmured something like, "Oh, yeah," but nobody heard him, which was lucky for him.

About the time she wrote "The Hero," Lucy prepared an article in connection with a study of weather. The children had chosen to record their findings in booklets, an idea that the classroom teacher encouraged because she knew the problems in expression that they would encounter. After Mr. A., the science teacher, demonstrated the making of a mercury barometer, they set to work readily enough, thinking it would be easy to write down what had happened. Soon, however, brows began to pucker, and one after another found himself unable to go on. Much of the difficulty lay, they concluded, in their lack of exact observation and understanding. So the demonstration was performed again, and points that had been vague were talked over. A second time they set to work at their writing, but they still found it an onerous task. Some gathered in small groups to read to one another and to ask for help on the parts that were not yet clear.

At length the teacher put Lucy's account on the board as an example of a lucid and complete explanation. Each child was allowed to check his own against it to see if he had included all of the essential information. The whole emphasis was on making the report as accurate as possible. Nothing was said about the abrupt beginning or the short, jerky sentences. Such awkward expression invariably occurs when children start writing in a new field. They feel the same lack of sureness that an artist feels when he undertakes working in a new medium. Fluency of expression comes only after much experience in this different way of thinking, and writing at this point can serve best by revealing the inadequacies in that thinking. As the ideas and relationships become more familiar, an improved sentence structure will reflect that better understanding. This we know from our experience. Here is Lucy's article:

Making a Mercury Barometer

Mr. A—— filled a tube with mercury. The tube was about 36 inches long. One end of the tube was sealed as in picture A. No air was in the tube. Next Mr. A——put some mercury in a bowl. The bowl was about 1/3 full. Next he put his finger over the open end of the tube, turned it upside down, and put the open end into the bowl. It was quite difficult because the mercury tried to escape. No air got in because the end of the tube was in the mercury. Then the mercury escaped into the bowl as far as it could against the pressure of the air, as in picure B. No air could have gotten into the space at the top. So all that was in there was a vacuum. Mercury is very heavy. Vacuum has no power. When the tube was full, it was heavier than air. But when the four inches of mercury escaped, it was no longer heavier. The air and the mercury in the tube went down as far as it could against the pressure of the air. The air was pushing all around as in picture C, trying to get into the vacuum. In pushing down on the mercury in the bowl it held up the mercury in the tube.

Through the six years we watched Lucy's growth with justifiable delight. From a shy little girl who flamed with embarrassment at the slightest provocation, she developed into a poised and able child. Many factors contributed to this wholesome change, not the least of which was the satisfaction and approval that came to her through her story writing. Because the stories she wrote were so intimate a creation, she felt that their warm reception was a reception of herself. Slowly but steadily she grew in assurance and self-esteem. Furthermore, the rich quality of her writing was a quickening force that gave impulse and direction to writing improvement in her group. We frankly admit that it is such workers as she who do our most fruitful teaching.

But I did see this — that like a carpenter who makes a table, a man who has written a poem has written it like that on purpose.
— WALTHER DE LA MARE, Come Hither

SIXTH CASE STUDY — PAT

From the beginning a certain neat directness was characteristic of Pat and all his work. In science and arithmetic he showed remarkable precision even at eight years. Interestingly enough, his art work was definitely superior and was characterized by the counterpart of this precision. His use of color was surprisingly exact and all his art products were distinguished by a strong sense of design. In contract to Ruth's uncertainty and fearfulness were Pat's clean-cut sense of direction and his economical route to achievement. Though not outstanding in ability, his sureness of approach and his selection of significant detail gave power to everything he wrote.

In the following story, written at eight, **is evidence of his** thrifty style.

Little Rabbit

Once there was a little rabbit. One day he went down to the river to get a drink. On the way he met a fox. Now this was a very wicked fox. He had tried to catch little rabbit and now he had him. The fox sprang. Little rabbit tried to run, but the fox was too quick for him. The fox took little rabbit to his den. Then the fox tried to eat little rabbit. But when he had his hands on him little rabbit bit him. Then the fox screamed. So at last the fox let him go and never tried to catch him again.

This story had several errors in sentence structure and in spelling, which was — and still is — Pat's Waterloo. However, the tale served its immediate purpose: the group was entertained and Pat was pleased.

During the following year increasing experience in the practical phases of writing provided both the necessity and the opportunity for correcting mechanics. It was characteristic of Pat's whole make-up that he should assimilate most of these skills quickly and thoroughly. He did all the required writing with ease, but never produced an abundance of personal writing. Perhaps this was due in part to his ability to express himself effectively in the field of art.

Pat was nine when he wrote "Mr. Ghost's Night Out." This story shows a decided growth in his particular narrative style and increased facility in the mechanics of writing. Several errors in spelling have been corrected.

Mr. Ghost's Night Out

One night Mr. Ghost sneaked out to play poker with the other ghosts. They played about two hours. Then Mr. Ghost looked at the clock. He snatched his hat from the post and ran home. But meanwhile Mrs. Ghost had found out he had gone and grabbed her rolling-pin and started out to look for him. About halfway between the two houses they met. And in the dim light Mrs. Ghost saw a dark figure of Mr. Ghost. But she did not know who it was. A terrified look came over her face. She let out a scream and threw up her hands. The rolling-pin went sailing into the bushes and away she went yelling and screaming blue murder. However she got home. Mr. Ghost ran home a different way. They got home at the same time. When Mr. Ghost came in Mrs. Ghost told all about what had happened and Mr. Ghost patted her on the back and said, "Don't worry. I'll protect you," and he took her off to bed.

Even though "Mr. Ghost's Night Out" is a much more ample tale than "Little Rabbit," its greater length is due to a larger concept of plot and not to superfluous detail. Note the incident in which "Mr. Ghost looked at the clock." Pat leaves interpretation to his audience but chooses significant detail from which the reader can sketch the rest of the picture. Again, in the ending, Pat has avoided the trivial, which clutters up much of children's writing.

Naturally in this group there were many occasions for letter writing. Pat was especially adept at this, for letter writing implies addressing one's ideas to a particular audience — in itself a selective process — and as you have observed, a precise choice of idea is the essence of Pat's style. Here is a letter written when Pat was ten. Note the choice of telling detail and the richness of implication in its placement.

> 7 Corning Road
> Bronxville, N. Y.
> May 19, 1937

Dear Uncle John,

We had an art exhibit in school. We hung all our pictures we had made this year in our classroom or in the halls. Most of the children made clay models, too. These we put in glass cases in the halls or laid them on the ledges in our room. All the children in my class made a picture of either an imaginary or a real flower. The day after our mothers came we went around to the different groups to

see the other classes' pictures. The sixth grade in my opinion had
the best ideas but they didn't always have the best painting.

I hope that you are much better now and that you will soon be
able to be out again.

Love,

PAT

Of course, this is a real letter of which the second draft was
actually sent to Uncle John.

Writing, both practical and personal, increased rapidly in
amount throughout the fifth and sixth grades. Only a fraction
can even be sampled here. The following report is one of
several that Pat wrote, but is reproduced here because it shows
a danger signal. Pat's power of selection when confronted with
a wide and somewhat confusing array of material produced this
inadequate and telescopic report.

Automobiles

One of the first attempts to drive a carriage by steam was made by
Captain Nicholas Joseph Cughot in 1769. By 1830 England had developed a steam carriage that could travel at ten miles per hour and
safely ascend and descend hills.

Two-thirds of the automobiles made in America are produced
in Michigan, Ohio, and Indiana. Great centers are Detroit, Lansing,
Pontiac, Cleveland, South Bend, and Connersville. The reason
Detroit is a great manufacturing city is because it has cheap lake
transportation, plenty of iron and steel, and good hardwood forests
near by. In recent years there were 25,000,000 automobiles in the
United States which is over four-fifths of the automobiles in the
world. Our motor vehicles include 25,500,000 passenger cars and
3,500,000 motor trucks. In Michigan in 1933 there were twenty-
four establishments manufacturing automobiles, having 59,725 em-
ployees earning in wages $66,675,000, and having an output valued
at $588,302,000. Not all factories make the same part of an auto-
mobile: for instance, some factories make only batteries. Then we
say that they specialize in making batteries.

In a factory there are many workers. Each worker has his own
job in manufacturing an automobile. If he does not get it done on
time, the car goes on to the next worker for him to do his job.

When the car reaches the end of the assembly line a man drives it out to test it. Then it goes to the dealer who sells the car.

REFERENCES

Automobiles from Start to Finish, pp. 3-56
The United States in the Modern World, pp. 186, 187
Our World, p. 145
Living in the Age of Machines, p. 262
Economic and Social Geography, pp. 563, 567, 569

Pat did not need much help either from his class or from his teacher to see that his report left too much to an uninformed audience. He sensed, also, that he had not sufficiently understood and digested his material to use it in following his plan of sequence. This was due in part to his use of too difficult reference material. A later report on armor, for which appropriate references were available, shows a reasonably thorough assimilation of facts and a more adequate presentation. A portion of this report is quoted here:

An armorer also made suits for knights to wear under their armor. To make a suit of mail the armorer took a small iron bar. This he heated and pounded until it was like a fine wire. Then he wound it around a small stake so that it took the shape of a circle. At that point he cut the wire into a link the ends of which he flattened and pierced and fastened together with a tiny nail. Often the nail was not larger than the head of a pin. When one link was fastened another was put through it and fastened in the same way. A shirt in a museum was estimated to have a hundred thousand links in it.

This paragraph contains facts garnered from three references, but Pat's increasing skill in selecting detail plus his realization of the dangers of telescoping material has produced a clear and interesting picture.

One of the last stories Pat wrote in the sixth grade may well be contrasted with "Little Rabbit," for in it one can mark the same qualities, though strengthened and expanded, that were lightly indicated in that early story.

One day on the beach of Plome Island a white speck was sighted not far from land. As it came closer the bathers realized that it was a sea monster. From the water women's screams pierced the air. For days no one ventured near the water until one day when there was no speck in sight, two men went in and swam out quite far. Then one of the men whose name was Joshua felt something very slimy against his legs. Now he was quite a show-off on shore with his loud bathing suit but in the water with this thing around his feet he sang a different tune. "Help," spluttered the unfortunate man, at the same time floundering wildly. His companion, seeing the antics of his friend, thought he was crazy and started swimming for shore as fast as he could. Meanwhile Joshua saw that the thing was slowly but surely coming to the surface of the water. When it came up far enough for him to see it plainly he found it was a dead shark. Seeing that it could do him no harm he turned it toward shore and was highly praised for his work. It was later found out that the "sea monster" was this dead shark because when a fish is dead it floats with its stomach up so that the white speck that was supposed to be the sea monster was the dead shark Joshua found floating around beyond the breakers.

Pat's own neat way of telling a story has remained unchanged during the three years since "Little Rabbit," but time has brought growth and refinement of his style. Contrast, for instance, the characterizations "a very wicked fox" and "He was quite a show-off on the shore with his loud bathing suit. . . ." Both are quick, but the latter is subtle as well. The same direct, economical narration, the thrifty choice of detail, the same quick characterization that we have noted will no doubt always distinguish Pat's writing, for they are as much a part of Pat as his straight back and steady blue eyes.

For out of the abundance of the heart the mouth speaketh. — St. Matthew, XII, 34

SEVENTH CASE STUDY — SARAH

Sarah was indeed a rare child. Seldom does one meet a person of so many dimensions. Physically large, often clumsy, interested and able in almost every field, whether artistic or academic, Sarah radiated a generous warmth that permeated all she did and fairly engulfed her friends and associates. She wrote copiously and, as you will see, well. She was gifted in music, studied both piano and violin, sang well, and had an unusually acute ear. Sarah's greatest love was for dramatics. She had an amazing insight into human nature and unusual power to create and interpret a wide variety of characters. Superior ability in art was but another gift in this extraordinary constellation.

Intellectually Sarah was also richly endowed and she explored each new world of ideas as zestfully as she would hurl herself into a game. This verve was coupled with almost irrepressible high spirits, which made Sarah an unusually delightful person. But sometimes her joyous headlong pace, joined with a complete disregard for the value of material things, wearied her teacher and companions. Sarah, for instance, had great difficulty learning to keep her belongings or even to put her desk in order. Nevertheless, she welcomed severe correction with the same generous spirit that prompted her to give away her best automatic pencil! Quick to sense a dramatic situation and eager to be a part of it, Sarah got into and out of an unusual number of childish scrapes. Her abundant sympathies were at once a strength and a potential danger.

Though absent more than half of her third school year, Sarah was one of the first to turn from storytelling to story writing. Even at this early age she showed keen invention and a flair for the dramatic, as can be seen in the following story. We have added some of the quotation marks and corrected the paragraphing.

A Story

Once there was a poor little boy. His name was Bobby. Bobby wanted to go to the circus. But he didn't have any money. His father was dead, he lived all alone with his mother. The circus had come to town that day and Bobby's heart was set on going. He had never been to one before. The boys on the block said it was wonderful. He asked his mother whether she would give him twenty-five cents to go to the circus.

"My son," she would say, weeping, "you ought to be glad you have bread and butter."

The next day Bobby went near the tents. He was just going to go in when a rough hand grabbed him. "Give me your money," said the man. And before Bobby could say "Jack Robinson" he landed neatly on the hard ground.

That night Bobby asked his mother whether he could get a job at the circus.

"Yes," was her reply.

The next morning Bobby got dressed and ran down to the circus grounds. Again the gruff man asked what he wanted there. "I want a job," Bobby replied.

"All right, what's your name?"

"My name is Bobby. What's yours?"

"My name is Bill. The manager is over there."

That afternoon Bobby White, for that was his name, came rushing home.

"Mother," he said, jumping and shouting, "I got a job at the circus and I can see the show free."

"But what do you do? How much pay do you get?" his puzzled mother asked.

"I carry water for the animals and I get twenty dollars a week."

Bobby went to the circus.

The dramatic quality of this situation and the method of its resolution are too obvious to need pointing out. And even at eight, Sarah enjoyed a cleverly turned phrase and graphic word, as in the sentences:

"His puzzled mother asked. . .," and " 'My son,' she would say, weeping, 'you ought to be glad you have bread and butter.' "

At nine Sarah was writing copiously. But in addition to rich invention and dramatic quality other essentials of good writing began to appear. For instance, contrast the structure of the first three sentences of Sarah's circus story with the first three sentences of "The Wormy Snake." Sarah was already alert to balance of sentence arrangement and quite unconsciously made use of a delightful cadence or euphonious quality in her choice of word and phrase. Note also Sarah's gleeful observation in the instance of Snapper's confession of what had not even been noticed by the unobservant school marm! Only two minor corrections in mechanics have been made.

The Wormy Snake

High in the tree-tops Miss Songster called all her pupils to singing class. One by one they came, Jenny Wren, Bob White, Jr., Cluck Cluck, Peep Peep, and many others. After all the rest were there, in walked Snapper.

"Snapper," said Miss Songster's sharp voice, "Why are you so late?"

"I — er — fell down."

"Well, never mind. I am going to call the cards."

Nobody liked singing lessons, especially the boys. But they couldn't play hookie because if anyone was absent Miss Songster would call up their mothers and ask them if their child was sick. If the mother said no, then when the children came home they would get a spanking.

But Snapper had a little scheme of his own. After the roll was called Miss Songster didn't pay any attention to the children. He sneaked out while she wasn't looking. When he was out of sight he thought he'd dig for a worm. He did not have to dig because there was one right on the ground in front of him. It was a great big one, too. He tried to pick it up. It was too heavy. The animal turned around. Snapper saw what a mistake he had made. It was a Rattlesnake. Snapper had been strictly warned about snakes.

He flew back to the schoolhouse with unusual speed. Snapper confessed everything. Miss Songster was a bit puzzled. She had not yet noticed Snapper's absence and she was surprised he confessed.

Snapper is now the best singer in Birdland and he doesn't mistake snakes for worms.

During the fifth grade the group was hit by an epidemic of mystery stories, and Sarah produced one as bloodcurdling and stereotyped as all the others, but still marked by a rich flow of language and by varied techniques of characterization.

Sarah, like many other children, got a positive glee from inventing preposterous names, as indicated in the following excerpt from a fifth-grade story:

Oscar (Oscar Aloysius Wurtelstein) being the ambitious type of brat suggested that we try a few of Timothy's (Timothy Potomus Bethybotom) father's precious fifteen-cent cigars.

Oscar, I take it, was not accustomed to this form of a delightful afternoon.

Cuspert and I lighted our cigars together. Cuspert took a terrific draw, (this is the first time he ever tried it) but managed to live through it. We sat for a few minutes calmly puffing while Oscar, Jedzercuss, and Timothy were half asleep in the lubber's hole. I was sitting there smoking and looking at the river when there was a terrific BANG!

The world was dead to all. . . .

Now this is, of course, a very poor tale. And the whole story is no better than the excerpt indicates. But even a superior child seldom travels an unbroken course from triumph to greater triumph. Moreover, it becomes increasingly obvious to us that children do gain something worthwhile from writing even such a yarn as that of Aloysius! Fluency, flexibility, a certain abandon seem to be achieved only from quantities of writing. Sarah, like others in her group, wrote increasingly in the fifth grade, and much of the product is distinguished by nothing more outstanding than an ever-widening vocabulary.

At the end of the fifth grade Sarah's group was asked to try doing personal editions of an old and well-known fable. Though this is an experiment that must be used infrequently, it provides opportunity to see individual style. Sarah's wealth of imagination and dramatic sympathy began to take on a certain subtlety of expression and a rather mature quality of implication, which can be seen especially in the conversation in the following story. This story also shows superior control of form. No changes have been made.

Toads and Diamonds

Once upon a time there was a widow with two daughters. One of these was just like her mother, ugly not only in facial expression but in temper also. The youngest however was just like her dead father, pretty, generous and had a good temper. Since the eldest was the very image of her mother naturally she was the favorite of the two. The mother made the youngest daughter do all the hard work and worst of all sent her to a well one and a half miles away twice a day with a tankard. One day when she was getting water she saw a beggar boy trying to get a drink with his cap but it all leaked out and the poor boy couldn't get any. The girl (whose name was Janice) being very courteous offered him some water out of the tankard. The boy accepted the drink readily. But as she held the tankard for the boy it grew heavier and it burned her fingers but she still hung on to it.

"May I have another drink?" asked the boy.

"You drink a lot for a boy your size. You may have another drink," replied the girl.

As you know by now, the boy was a fairy trying to find if the girl was really courteous. This time the tankard was very heavy and it burned more than ever. When the boy finished he threw down the tankard and he turned into a glamorous lady with a wand in her hand.

"Janice," she said, "you gave me water when you thought I was thirsty even if it was heavy and it burned you. I shall reward you with a lovely gift. Whenever you speak either jewels or flowers will come out of your mouth."

Janice was so bewildered that she ran all the way home without the water or the tankard. When she got home her mother yelled at her and said, "Stupid! Why have you been so long and where is the water? And the tankard?"

"I'm so sorry," said Janice. And three roses and four diamonds came out of her mouth.

"My dear child, how did this happen?" (This was the first time she had called her 'My dear child.') "Fannie, my little pet, see what has happened to your sister because she went to the well to draw water. Janice, how did this befall you, darling?"

Janice told the story simply and truthfully.

"Fannie," cried her mother, "take a pail and if you see that boy, treat him civilly."

"I'll look like a fine how-do-you-do drawing water," answered Fannie and after much grumbling she departed with a golden pitcher.

When she got to the well she saw a tall thin lady with a crown on her head, undoubtedly of some high rank. But it was really the fairy trying to find out how far the girl's ugliness would go. Fannie started to draw water when the tall lady asked for a drink of it.

"Did your Grace think that this pitcher was for the use of every person who comes along? However, here is some," Fannie threw the whole vaseful at the lady and dropped the golden pitcher which broke instantly. The princess suddenly turned into the fairy.

"For your meanness, I shall give you a gift. Whenever you speak either a snake or a viper will come out of your mouth."

"Humph," said Fannie. A snake came out of her mouth and she went home. When she got there her mother said:

"Tell me what happened, sweet, and I'll count the jewels that come out of your mouth."

"It's all that miserable creature's fault," said Fannie (a lizard and a viper came out of her mouth), "and that horrible witch's!" And she told the whole story.

By the time she was through the kitchen floor was full of snakes and toads and lizards. The widow gave Janice a beating and turned her out of the house. Janice wandered into the woods and lay down and cried. Now the sovereign of the country who happened to be coming back from a fox hunt, saw this fair girl weeping on the ground and asked her what was wrong. Janice told him how her mother had turned her out (not sparing the jewels and flowers). The king was very angry and wanted the wicked mother and daughter executed but Janice, being very kind, would not have it. The king took her to his palace and there they were married and lived happily ever after.

Space prohibits the inclusion of any other fifth-grade writing, personal or practical. But Sarah, of course, did the expected amount of writing of letters, records, brief reports, and shared in the preparation of a science book about trees for a second grade in school. The latter offered an excellent opportunity to practice simple, clear writing. And considerable practice was needed! The entire group profited much from the discipline of exact expression and continuity of organization.

During the sixth grade momentum increased tremendously, partly, we believe, because the prewriting stages of development had been richly explored. Though Sarah wrote frequently with a partner or two, only a few examples of her individual writing are shown here. When the sixth-grade group was making a series of industrial studies in geography, Sarah chose to study oranges and wrote an extended report noteworthy for its improvement in organization.

Another piece of work done by Sarah during her sixth year was entirely self-chosen. She had visited Austria at one time and had heard much about the days of the "dual monarchy," a phrase in which she took delight. With the class she keenly enjoyed hearing Kate Seredy's *White Stag,* and brought her own copy to school to hold and look at while the teacher finished reading the last chapters. When the class was studying medieval life, any reference to the Huns was sure to evoke some special response from Sarah. Her report was heartily enjoyed by the class, and Sarah was so excited that she had twisted herself from one side of the classroom to the other by the time she had finished reading it aloud. An excerpt follows:

The Huns

There are few certain facts known about the early Huns. In medieval books (which are very few) they were only spoken of unfavorably.

The Huns were very small in stature but their bones were strong. They also were very quick on their feet. These small men often had to endure unimaginable hardships. A Hun sometimes lived on his horse for days. This made him bow-legged. His broad face, large ears and slit-eyes half scared people out of their wits. He had no hair on his face except perhaps for a fierce mustache. When they were babies hot irons were applied to their faces and all the hair on cheek and chin was burned out. That accounts for all the scars on their faces in later years. Another custom of the Huns was to wash each new born babe out in the open air (regardless of winter or summer) and give it a bath every day for forty-two days (six weeks). These were to last it for the rest of its life. Cattle could not stand the rough life the Hun led so he had to keep sheep and horses. Sometimes he had camels. His food consisted of milk products (preferably mares' milk) and sometimes horses' blood. They also ate half raw meat which they warmed by putting it between their and their horse's body. . . .

References are duly quoted by pages so that notes can be rechecked if necessary, a technique highly respected by Sarah and the whole group.

The last story written by Sarah in the sixth grade follows:

"I can't see," muttered Johnny Elephant, as he strutted before the reflecting waters of the mill-pond, "why all the girls of this village aren't in love with me, I being such a handsome young fellow."

So saying he reached into his back pocket, brought out his red bandana handkerchief and wiped his tusks. He then picked a white flower at the edge of the mill-pond and put it into the lapel of his little blue jacket. Then looking very important he put his hands into his pockets, held his head high and strutted down the road to Suzie May's house.

Splash! He had unexpectedly landed in a mudpuddle and a thin high-pitched voice was giggling from the house.

"Ha, ha! You — are funny," giggled Suzie May. . . .

The rest of the story develops the adventures of the young show-off elephant who finally ran away from home to make his fortune. Sarah ends the story thus:

It must have been around twelve o'clock when he woke up and found two shining eyes staring at him out of the darkness.

"Oh," he moaned, as he cuddled closer to the tree, "I want my mother."

"Boo—o—oo," went the voice of the owl, who was the owner of the two staring eyes.

Johnny did not hesitate for a moment. He leaped up and ran as fast as he could.

The next day Johnny ate off the mantlepiece.

The discernment of human frailties so whimsically treated in the adventures of Johnny Elephant is another evidence of the flowering of unusual gifts. Furthermore, one sees real growth in ease and flexibility of structure, in economy and subtlety of implication. It is also obvious that the needed discipline in skills and techniques has in no wise crippled the free play of an active imagination. It seems essential for us to preserve in any child that spontaneity so necessary for later development. Therefore, it is a matter of signal importance that Sarah, like less able children in her group, retained a delightful un-self-consciousness and a genuine zest to write simply for the joy of writing.

The art of life consists in creating an individual and a unique self. — POWYS, **A Philosophy of Solitude**

7. *Writing and Growth*

THE complete freedom necessary for the life of the creative spirit has always stood opposed to the methodical acquisition of English skills and techniques. Correctness has appeared the antithesis of spontaneity. That a more careful analysis of these antagonisms is needed has been deeply felt by many persons dealing with young children. That a more constructive synthesis could be made of these apparently disparate elements has been our guiding premise. To this end we have recorded our experience.

Long dissatisfied with the results of our teaching of writing we had through trial and error discarded at least a little of the empty ritual. A nucleus of common belief incited four of us to experiment more definitely along the lines of our emerging understanding. So with the happy accident of continuity of pupil groups we proceeded to test and to clarify our beliefs. These years of experience and study have led us to believe that

we have found a way to nurture the creative spirit and at the
same time to effect power in the use of writing skills. Gratifying
results have come from what we believe is a clear understanding
of the essential functions of written expression and of the natural tendencies of children's growth in relation to writing. It
appears that the utilitarian and artistic phases of writing are not
mutually antagonistic when the reality of the one and the
freedom of the other are zealously guarded.

BASIC BELIEFS

Writing, we believe, serves at least two needs for writer and
audience: that of artistic self-expression and that of communi-
cating functional ideas. One is personal, individual, imaginative, and highly perishable. The other is utilitarian, realistic,
or intellectual, and needs the discipline of correct mechanics to
be socially acceptable. The former seems to be kept alive best
by complete freedom to experiment and complete assurance of
a respectful reception of the product regardless of its nature. In
contrast to this the acquisition of form seems intrinsically a
function of that realistic writing wherein other people are practically concerned. Writing of this nature springs from sources
relatively constant; the need or authority remains as a point of
reference against which the product can be checked. The author
works more as a reproducer of known facts, conditions, or ideas,
presented, of course, in his unique fashion. But the material
recorded exists outside himself. Hence the writing is not so
intimately a part of the inner self. Correction and verification
can be required without the loss of an idea and without injuring
the individual. Moreover, these operations take time, and only
where the material is more nearly objective and the needs or
sources are rather permanent can time be taken to work over
and improve expression to say *exactly* what a writer needs to
say. Not so in personal writing where the sources lie almost
wholly within the individual and where there is no final authority other than personal taste. Time out to revamp inde-

pendent clauses may mean loss of the whole idea. Or of even more serious import, time out to edit story after story may so curb the swift imagination or so fatigue the uncertain and immature young writer that desire to write turns all too often to dread of writing. Confusion that arises from trying to shape child ideas to an adult's conception or pattern has resulted in mimicry or even in obvious plagiarism.

Furthermore, our experience indicates that the same literary designs that conscientious teachers would imprint, usually with deadening consequences, develop more vividly from inner necessity. When children write with the definite idea of enlisting the attention of an audience from the beginning to the end of an engaging tale, they learn in time to select that which gives vigor and spirit to their writing. To hold even a tolerant and friendly audience in gratifying suspense, a writer must really tell a story. Beginning with a propelling idea or suggestion, implying just enough probability of outcome to start the listeners' curiosity, opening several possible ways of working out a solution, holding the suspense to the very end — these and other elements are found by actual, personal trial to be effective techniques of story construction. Design thus emerges from the same story-teller-to-audience situations that have been the beginnings of our literary heritage. Writer, storyteller, and audience form an organic whole that operates naturally to strengthen and vitalize written expression. Indeed, rules of literary structure have come from just such reality, but they have been crystallized into academic principles that usually leave the young quite ignorant of their functional origin. The real situations that first produced those principles of structure need to be relived again and again by young writers. Continued experience in being sometimes a writer and frequently an avid listener can make an individual so sensitive to elements of story design that he naturally appropriates some of them for his own use. The delight of entertaining an audience with the magic of his own creation is a pleasure to be sought again and again. And satisfaction from such success begets even greater zest for writing.

Practical writing, too, makes its contribution to the balanced growth of writing power. When a child's first contacts with the art of writing have been truly meaningful to him, an effective beginning has been made. Situations so realistic that the results of a written communication are readily observable kindle a merited respect for writing as a means to action. This feeling of reality is essential; otherwise learning to write can become the merest muscular performance. But a skill that is significant in a child's important affairs has a far different future. For the person-to-person directness of most utilitarian writing necessitates that clarity which becomes the hallmark of fine exposition. Continued experience leads naturally from the most practical and necessary communication to the recording of worth-while discovery and experience. Striving for clarity and order in purposeful written expression fosters further respect for the effective economies and obligations of good utilitarian writing. In this more objective expression some success is possible for nearly all children. Many a youngster feels his first, perhaps his only, power over elusive words by producing an informational record that he is proud to call a book. Some children who cannot lose themselves in flights of invention find their greatest satisfaction in the graciously worded social letter or in the unmistakably clear explanation. For them, this is a real outlet, no less worthwhile than lyric, phantasy, or enchanting story. Individuality is just as likely to find expression here and to be further cultivated by such experience.

Standards of attainment, too, are more easily applied in the fields of practical writing than in those imaginative areas where the individual must be his own authority. A child can be more certain that his product is good in the usual, conventional sense. Direct teaching of some of the accepted forms of punctuation arrangement, and structure make children sure that what they have written will meet established standards. For some uncertain souls this assurance is necessary and productive of further strength in writing as well as further self-confidence and security. And for all, pride in workmanship, so often lacking in our age of ready-made commodities, can be a wholesome experience.

THE TEACHER'S ROLE

As we became aware of children's potentialities for growth in writing, we came to see our own responsibilities more clearly. The more we saw power emerging from the complementary experiences of practical and personal writing, the less we felt the need of pressing children to write. Children's response to their own purposes spurred them to more and better writing. Individual projection to an understanding audience was the basis of wholesome self-realization and a means to stronger, clearer written expression. Our role was the difficult one of establishing those situations that not only allowed for writing but that also fostered it and at times required it. Most important of all, we found ourselves responsible for the emotional climate in which creative insight deepened.

A second aspect of our teaching function came into sharper focus as we worked longer in the exact discipline of practical writing and the joyous expansion of personal writing. We could not adopt a *laissez faire* attitude of letting children grow. Rather, we had to sense when and how to introduce fresh experiences, to open new vistas in keeping with their developing capacities. This timing of new ventures was not easy. Depth of experience was more productive than a surfeit of new experiences, for the latter course resulted only in superficiality and indifference. Children need adults to bring them into effective relationship with new materials. Left to themselves their explorations lead to a thinning of content and a dulling of perception. Shared with a knowing adult, their efforts achieve a status that empowers them to reach out to new maturity. The direction of children's growth from dependence to independence is based in large part on adult dynamics.

GUIDING PRINCIPLES

The interaction between such practical and personal writing, slow but certain in its fulfillment, proceeds naturally for the enrichment of both. Again and again this mature integration has delighted us. Frequently the process has seemed slow, but out of a morass of trials, mistakes, disappointments, and rewards, some beliefs have been clarified for us into underlying essentials. Our four years of study and observation here described in concrete detail have led us to believe, tentatively at least, that growth proceeds best under certain productive conditions. These we attempt to predicate as guiding principles:

Because of physical immaturity a child's first handwriting should be restricted to those uses for which he sees a need.

During the early school years of limited writing ability a child's inventiveness and story feeling are fostered by frequent experiences in telling and in dictating.

Personal writing should not be expected until the child has had a wealth of satisfying experience with oral expression and has gained sufficient physical skill to prevent undue fatigue.

Each child's ability to express his ideas is distinctly unique and personal. The rate at which this ability grows is likewise individual. Only harm can come from trying to force more mature forms of expression than children show themselves ready to use.

From the beginning, practical writing must meet high standards of form and organization, which most children accept willingly because their writing serves a genuine use.

Personal writing needs to fulfill only the child's desires, except upon those extremely rare occasions when correct form is necessary out of consideration for others or when the product is to be permanently preserved.

It is equally important to accept a child's own form for his personal expression and to help him learn conventional forms for practical writing. Each experience contributes to the other, leading to a natural integration of style and technique as the writer matures.

Every child writes himself into his product. Style, tempo, phrasing, characterization, choice of subject are exponents of individual personality.

Since the child can write honestly only that which is truly his, time to assimilate experience and information is vitally necessary.

Exposure to fine literature contributes immeasurably to a

richer, more adequate expression. Conversely, the effort of trying to write one's own ideas effectively and colorfully heightens sensitivity to good literature.

Children's writing reflects the impact of such mass media as television, radio, comics, and movies, not only in vocabulary but also in tempo and characterization.

Personal writing serves the need for the release of tensions and for the draining of aggressions, fears, and destructive emotions.

If personal writing is to be kept a joyous and genuine outlet it cannot be strait-jacketed as to subject and form. When written expression is truly free and spontaneous all sorts of ideas and shades of feeling emerge. Stimulation or suggestion may give direction to some pupils at some times. But the human mind seems much too wayward to be confined in its artistic experimentation to a prescribed or given content. Even the child mind — perhaps even more certainly the child mind — is not likely to be spontaneous in verse or prose about a particular unit of study. The life of the spirit seems too profound to absorb into its inner realms very much of the academic learning exemplified in even the best schools. Only rarely does the elementary school child so thoroughly identify himself with a portion of the curriculum as to draw upon that experience in his personal writing. Much more fertile material for this field of creative endeavor is likely to arise from sources of which the most sensitive teacher is scarcely conscious, if at all. Individual impressions of the adult world, concealed desires well-cloaked behind natural or fantastic figures, naive reactions to what is taken for granted by grownups — these and many other strange avenues are likely to be used with perfect freedom. In children's personal writing, truly there can be no bounds, for each individual must speak from and for himself.

On the other hand, the immediate activities of the elementary school offer abundant opportunities for the exercising of utilitarian language. Clarity of structure, sound organization, and correct techniques are necessary aspects of a product to be shared with others. These elements learned in action become part of a child's working equipment. Teaching them in functional settings increases the efficiency with which they are learned.

Probably everyone who has experimented with children's creative enterprises has been amazed and deeply gratified to witness the tremendous energy and concentration which characterize such activity. This absorption with an idea, a dance, a picture, a story, a play, is too important an aspect of child life to be lightly treated. An activity that so genuinely engages the whole person and either thrills him with his success and prowess or irritates him with his failure leaves almost visible changes in that person, who for a while has lost himself in his adventure. For a time, at least, the adventure is all-important; the product with which he struggles banishes all self-consciousness. The creator is objectified in what he has produced. Perhaps because of this important quality of personal absorption in the job such creative outlet builds anew the child who, but a brief hour before, has been the builder. Where children are concerned, the rewards of creative action to the individual are more important than the excellence of the product. Seldom will even our most gifted children produce lasting works of art, and then only after considerable fumbling and mediocre output. But the growth of the personal entity, though immeasurable as yet by scientific procedures, defies negation. Those who have watched the process *know*. Those who have seen energy kindled and honest pride effected by creative effort with music, or poetry, or dance, or well-delivered research, have seen also a new and stronger person quicken into being.

This process of growth and creation, miraculous from the beginning, remains as mysterious as the original creation, upon which mankind has ever speculated. But the manifestations of this growth from the limitations of childhood to the full maturity of the articulate adult are discernible, though infinitely subtle and delicate. Children come slowly into their heritage of that most significant cultural tool by which man has recorded much of his intellectual and esthetic achievement. We have been privileged to study a process at once intriguing and elusive.

Appendix

Story Supplement

WE have found it helpful to have on hand a stockpile of
children's stories to be used for various purposes. Such a
collection is not an accumulation of the best stories but rather
a full cross section, including some that are meager, some that are
full of active aggression, and some that start with verve but are
unfinished. We have found we could never have too many
stories on hand, for that which "catches on" with one group
may fail to stir another.

From this collection we draw stories to read during the
"warming-up process" with a new group, or when a class is
caught on a plateau of writing and needs a lift to a new level, or
just for fun because children take such delight in them. Always
we read for stimulation and enjoyment, *never* to make overt
comparison or to present models to be copied.

The stories that follow are kinds we have found useful; they may serve as the beginning of a working collection.*

Jimmie's Stick

Jimmie had a little stick that was magic. And one day Jimmie wanted a dime.

He said, "Hocus pocus, let me have a dime."

And that second he had a dime. And he said it over and over again. And he got more and more money so that he can have ice cream and soda and candy and cake and all good things to eat. And he lived happy ever after.

                                                   A third-grade boy

There was a little bear. He did not have a name. People called him names and he punched them and sometimes he cried. And he tried and tried to get a name. But he cannot. So he sat down and he was thinking for days and soon he came to a name. It was "Fire."

And a fox asked him, "What is your name?"

He said, "Fire."

The fox said, "I can't hear you."

So he called out, "FIRE."

So all the animals in the jungle came and wanted to put out the fire.

His mother told four animals to come to the house. So they came. They sat down thinking. The four of them had a name and all of them had the same. The mother bear said to one, "Have you got a name?"

He said, "Bee."

"No, no," said the mother bear. "That ain't a name." So little bear started to cry.

Mother bear said, "Little bear, do not cry. You can go out if you like."

"I do not want to go out. All the animals will call me names." So he named himself "Monkey."

So the same fox asked him, "Have you got a name?"

He said, "Yes, I have."

So the fox said, "What is it?"

He said, "Monkey."

---

* To facilitate reading, spelling has been corrected and punctuation added. A few obviously omitted words have been inserted in brackets.

So the fox called out, "Foxes, come here. This little bear's name is 'Monkey'."

So all the foxes called out, "Oh, look at the monkey."

So he went home and told his mother and she named him "Tim" and he lived happy ever after.

An eight-year-old *

Buttercup Wilkins was a yellow cat, a really nice cat, but no one liked her. The other cats felt very uppity about her and never asked her to play with them. But Buttercup Wilkins didn't mind. She had fun by herself.

One day Priscilla Moore, a black cat with white paws, made some duckleberry jam. Duckleberry jam is very extra special good and she decided to have a party about it.

She said to the other cats, "Will you come to my house and play cards and have some of my duckleberry jam?"

They said, "Yes, but don't ask that Buttercup Wilkins."

"I won't," said Priscilla. "Come tomorrow at three."

But they didn't know that Buttercup Wilkins was hiding in the bushes beside them.

So the next afternoon Buttercup Wilkins watched the other cats go into the party. Then she slipped gently through the door into the pantry where the jam was. Without making a sound she quietly pawed out and ate every bit of that jam. She even put her nose in each jar and licked it shining.

Then Buttercup Wilkins slowly licked the jam from her face and paws. She carefully closed the door of the jam closet and wearing a smile at the edge of her whiskers, she slipped past all the mean chattering cats whose noses were all so uppity they did not even see her.

A third-grade girl

Bojo, the elephant, was talking to the man who ran the steam shovel. He wanted to take over his work for his lunch hour. He started to tell the man that he used to run a steam shovel himself. Of course it wasn't true.

"Well," said the man, "if you are sure you can do it ——."

"Of course I can do it." Of course he was talking through his hat.

---

* The eight-year-old who wrote this at the end of third grade was burdened with the name "Bodo." His original copy consists of but two run-on sentences. As he read the tale his voice indicated the punctuation we have used here.

Then Bojo climbed into the steam shovel and began to pick the dirt. Suddenly the clutch flew back. He lost control of the steering wheel. The steam shovel turned over and Bojo was underneath.

Then the man came running. "Now look what you've done."

Bojo slowly got out of the pieces that used to be the steam shovel. The manager called the police. The police [came] with sirens ringing. The police grabbed Bojo. There was a barbed wire fence close by the policeman and Bojo headed for it. The policeman [turned] around and Bojo gave him a big push into the fence.

The policeman shouted, "OW! My seat!"

Bojo ran away and Bojo never, never said that he could run a steam shovel again.

A third-grade girl

Window Trouble

Mo and Nig, the play dectectives, were washing the windows of their house when they broke a window.

Nig said, "I think we had better get out of here."

"So do I," said Mo.

So Nig hid behind the water barrel and Mo climbed up the drain pipe only to find Mother Bear climbing up the other side.

"Here comes Mom," said Mo and he slid down the roof, BUT he forgot Nig! Down the drain pipe he went and right into Nig's lap.

"Nice landing," said Nig as Mo got up.

Just then Uncle Upper Bumper heard the noise. Around the corner came a big fat stomach, then a very little head and a big twenty-five gallon hat.

"Well," said Uncle Upper Bumper, "a fine mess! Two little bears nice and wet! I thought you were washing the windows."

"You think too much," said Nig very softly.

That was too much for Uncle Upper Bumper. He called Mrs. W. Y. L. P. Q. Bear to spank them.

Nig said, "Get us out of this, Dectective Mo."

"Shut up! You know I can't," said Mo.

"Here comes Mom," said Nig softly.

"We were — er — washing the windows and we had a little trouble," said Mo. "Nig dropped the pail of water on my head and I fell and Nig slipped on the water that spilled."

"A very good story. Is it true?"

"Oh, yes," said the two bears.

"O. K., here's fifty cents to go to the movies."

In five minutes they were in sight of the movies. "I'm glad we got out of that one," said Nig.

Meanwhile at home — "This ought to fix them," said Mother Bear. "This is a new lie detector machine."

Just then Uncle Upper Bumper came into the room. "What a nice chair," he said. (The chair was the lie detector machine.) "And a very comfortable one at that."

Just then the two bears came in very tired and they went right up stairs and went to sleep.

A third-grade boy

Mud and Tud

Mud and Tud were two ducks that lived in Mrs. Hakelman's house in the ice box. They liked the cold spots. Mr. Hakelman is mayor of the town and is going to give a ball. Mrs. Hakelman has had to bake some cakes. She has laid them in the ice box on the second shelf down.

It happened to be that Mud and Tud were on the top shelf. Mud was holding Tud's hand. All of a sudden Mud slipped and they both went down. They landed right beside a huge cake which towered above them. It had three layers. Mud and Tud started to eat their way in. Luck was with them. The icing dripped down to cover the hole.

Mrs. Hakelman came home about four o'clock. "A-a-a-a-a, my cakes seem to be ready. Now to take them to the ball. Oh cook, oh cook! Oh, there you are. Take these cakes to the car."

PART TWO: *At the Ball*

The thirteenth piece of cake was passed to Mrs. Bradley, the fattest lady in town. All of a sudden out jumped Mud and Tud. Mrs. Bradley SCREAMED.

A third-grade boy

Taffy Tugboat

Taffy Tugboat was in the dock when an ocean liner came in to dock in some fog and bumped Taffy Tugboat 'way under the dock. Taffy Tugboat was stuck. Taffy Tugboat tooted his whistle but nobody came to help him.

Now Taffy Tugboat was in a mess. He tugged and pulled but he could not get out. What would his master say? He would be very angry if he was not there to take him out to the big boats to pull them in.

He had to get out from under that dock. All of a sudden he heard two men coming over the dock. He tooted his whistle. The two men heard him. They were scared. They ran to the police. They said a big monster was under the dock in a very big rage and if he wasn't caught he would try to control the whole city.

The whole police department went to the dock very quietly and started to shoot at the dock. Taffy Tugboat now was in a mess.

All of a sudden the shooting stopped. A man said that he thought that what they were shooting at was not a monster. It was his tugboat and it *was his boat.* It was Taffy Tugboat.

A third-grade boy

Fuzzy Gets in Trouble

Bang! Bang! Bang! There was an awful racket coming from the cellar. "Ow-w, my thumb!" Fuzzy and Billy Rabbit were making a wagon.

"Whew, thank goodness, that's done! Now let's play in it."

"Yes, let's coast down the hill by Mr. Snobbottom's house."

"O.K., but we won't be able to make any noise," said Fuzzy.

"Why not?"

"Because he'll bawl us out."

"Yeah, I guess so."

"Well, come on," said Fuzzy, pulling the wagon out of the yard. "Whee-e, boy is this fun? Hey, Billy, I can't steer."

"Help, we're going right into Mr. Snobbottom's yard," yelled Billy.

"Yes, and the drive's just been cemented."

"Get out of my new driveway," bawled Mr. Snobbottom.

"We can't," wailed Fuzzy.

"Why not?" yelled Mr. Snobbottom.

"Because we're stuck in the cement."

"Well, get out anyway. Walk off. You can get the wagon later," he yelled, "but get off my new driveway!"

"O.K." said Billy, climbing out of the wagon. Fuzzy climbed out too.

"HELP!" yelled Fuzzy.

"Help!" echoed Billy.

"Oh, I can't walk. I'm cemented in," wailed Fuzzy.

"So'm I," cried Billy.

Then the front door opened and Mr. Snobbottom waddled out of the house, for he was very fat. "Well, why don't you take off your shoes?"

"O.K. Now we're stuck again."

"Well, take off your socks."

"I can't because they're wet," said Billy.

"Oh, I'll get them off for you," said Mr. Snobbottom, walking onto the cement. He had gone a few steps when he let out a yell. "HELP! I'm stuck too!" Then he forgot all about being scared and started bawling Fuzzy and Billy out. "I'll get the police on you if I have to use hounds."

"First you'll have to get a tow truck," said Fuzzy under his breath.

Now really Fuzzy and Billy were on a dry part of the driveway, but Mr. Snobbottom wasn't. So Fuzzy and Billy just walked away laughing.

BUT (a small word with a big meaning) the next day Mother Rabbit opened the door on a much battered-up cross man. "Mrs. Rabbit, I demand to take your son to the police."

"Why — what do you mean?" asked Mother Rabbit, a bit astonished.

"Just what I said," and he told the story.

BANG! The front door slammed in his face. He was so astonished he lay down and died; so that was the end of Mr. Snobbottom.

THE END

A fourth-grade boy

Clean Hands and a Pure Heart

Tommy Rabbit tried to sit down at the table without being noticed by his mother. But she saw him all right.

"Let me see them," she said.

Tommy showed her his right hand which was pretty clean.

"Now the other," she said.

He had to show her his left hand which had a big ink spot on it.

"Now, Tommy Rabbit," said his mother, "you know better than to come to the table with hands like that, especially today when all the mothers are going to school for a program. You go right up stairs and wash them again."

Tommy went upstairs grumbling to himself about how silly grown-ups were about clean hands. While he was upstairs he got an idea. That bad little rabbit tip-toed into his mother's room and there was her hat and her gloves laid out for the program at school. Very quietly Tommy put a lot of black powder from his chemistry set into each glove. Then he washed his hands and went downstairs.

After lunch Mrs. Rabbit put on her hat and pulled on her gloves and started off with Tommy. While they were walking along,

Tommy picked up some stones and a piece of dirty string and in no time his hands were dirty again. Of course, Mrs. Rabbit had to notice that.

"Tommy," she said, "you will be the death of me. Look at your hands."

"Oh, well, Mother," said Tommy, "boys always have dirty hands."

"No," said Mrs. Rabbit, "your father never had dirty hands and anyway I always say, 'Clean hands and a pure heart.' I am very careful to see that MY hands are always clean." When she said this Tommy began to cough and look up at the sky.

When they got to the school, Miss Fluffy, the teacher, came out to meet all the mothers. Mrs. Rabbit pulled off her glove as she shook hands with Miss Fluffy. Of course, her hand was black with the powder and in a minute so was Miss Fluffy's. Neither of them noticed it because they were so busy shaking hands with the other mothers.

Suddenly Mrs. Rabbit looked down at her black paws.

"Oh, my heavens," she said and fainted.

When she came to, Tommy said, "You had better go right upstairs and wash your hands, Mother. How about clean hands and a pure heart?"

And from that day Mrs. Rabbit was never quite so fussy about Tommy's dirty hands.

A fourth-grade boy

Spanked Too Many Times

"Goodby, Mother," said the five bears. They were going away to Grandma's farm.

The five bears got on the train and waved until the train was out of sight. Then Mother Bear went into the station to send a telegram to Grandma. Mr. Brown the telegraph man was a very good friend of Mother Bear.

"Hello, Mr. Brown," said Mother Bear. "Nice morning, isn't it."

"Yep," said Mr. Brown.

"Can I send a telegram now?" said Mother Bear.

"Yep," said Mr. Brown.

This is what Mother Bear said in the telegram:

DEAR MOTHER,

I am sending my five little children. I hope they're going to have a nice time.

Your loving daughter,
ANNABELLE

R.S.V.P.

Mother Bear said to Mr. Brown, "Can I wait for the answer?"

"Yep," said Mr. Brown.

The answer came and this is what it said: "OH NO! — MOTHER."

Mr. Brown giggled. "I have a feeling they're going to be home pretty soon."

But up on Grandma's farm we find our five heroes having to have a pail of water thrown on their seats. "I'll get even with Grandma for this," said Nig.

Later we find them toasting marshmallows twenty years old that Grandma's husband gave her as an only wedding present. Grandma was shopping, but not for long because she had met Reverend Jones running down the street toward the fire station.

"What's wrong?" said Grandma.

"My prize rosebush is on fire."

With that Grandma knew something was very wrong. She hurried home to find nobody there. But when she got out in the backyard she could hardly keep herself from screaming. Her best sheet was on fire. The Bears didn't know she was there. But they did when she took them by the ears and reddened their seats.

A few hours later they were home and taking turns sliding down the rain pipe into the water barrel.

"You and your Big Ideas," said Mo to Nig.

Splash — Blub — Blub.

A fourth-grade girl

California or Bust

One summer morning Eenie, Meenie, Meinie, Mo, and Nig started out. Each had a bundle under their arm. Nig was the last. On his back hung a sign, "California or Bust." As they went along a tribe of Indians came down the hill. Nig was last and an Indian caught him and took him home to the tribe. They put him in a big pot. They were just ready to cook him when there was a big noise. The Bears had put a jazz record on the victrola and were playing it full blast. The Indians went over to see what the noise was. Meanwhile the bears untied Nig.

Meanwhile at home Mother Bear said, "Such peace and quiet without those pesty bears."

The next morning Mother Bear went into Eenie, Meenie, Meinie, Mo, and Nig's room. She almost fainted. There in bed were Eenie, Meenie, Meinie, Mo and Nig. On the bed hung a sign:

"WE BUSTED!"

A fourth-grade girl

Nig's Horse

Eenie, Meenie, Meinie, Mo and Nig were packing their bags for a summer in the West. Nig had been waiting for this moment all during winter, so you can imagine how long he had waited. At last it was time to say "farewell" to the winter house, and "Howdy" to the West. It took them two whole days to get there.

About every five minutes of the trip Mama Bear would look back and check up on her children and say, "How are my little honey dumplings back there?"

Every time Nig said, "Be quiet! Can't you tell that I'm trying to see which one of my fifteen cowboy suits I'm goin' to wear first?"

When they got to the house in which they were going to stay in, Nig immediately ran upstairs to change into a cowboy suit. "Why in such a hurry?" asked Mama Bear.

"Don't ask such silly questions," said Nig. "Can't you see by the way I'm dressed that I'm goin' horseback ridin'?"

"Well, Mr. Smartypants, whose horse are you going to use?" said Mama.

"I didn't think of that yet," said Nig.

Later, after an hour of housecleaning Nig discovered a television set. Since Nig had never heard or seen a television set, he just so happened to turn it to Channel Four. There he saw a man on a beautiful white horse. Nig was interested. I will now tell you what was happening on television.

"Bang! Bang! Bang! Ugh! He got me, Hoppie." The story was about Hopalong Cassidy, John Jenkins and California. Just then Hoppie got off his horse, and well, that was Nig's chance. Crash! Bang! The set was broken, and so was Nig!

                                                             A fourth-grade girl

"Wham" went the door of the Bear home. "Ma," cried Nig and Mo together. "Ma, can we have the living room for our club?"

"Well — " said Mother Bear.

"*Please,* Mom."

"Well — all right."

"Yippy," cried Mo and Nig. "Let's tell the gang."

Next day the five bears were decorating the living room. Nig and Mo were giving orders. In two more days the living room was a sight. The wall paper had been peeled off and in its place were crayon Indians drawn by Mo. The drapes had been pulled together and the room was very dark. The carpets had been rolled up and sheets had been put in their place. All the tables and chairs in the house were put in rows and Eenie was getting the gang together.

All this time Father Bear was away (Thank Goodness!). But the *day* the first meeting was to be held was the day father was to come home. Father opened the door of his home to find the living room in the sight it was. Father grabbed all five bears BUT Mother Bear saved the bears from a sore seat that night by telling father. *And* Father saved the bears from another sore seat. Because if Mother had heard what kind of a club the Bears were running, she would have spanked them.

P.S. The bears were talking about cookies and cake and ice cream. (at the club meeting) They were going to take them from Mother Bear. She was making them for the County Bazaar.

A fourth-grade pupil

Arthur Finds an Unhappy Home

Arthur, the ant, was pacing the floor of his old home in the pig pen. He was thinking of how bad the housing shortage was. Who wanted to live in a pig pen? He positively did not.

Arthur said to himself, "I'll go out and look for a new house."

After four days of looking he was packed up and living in a new home. Now all he needed was a wife but all his friends tried to warn him by saying, "All you'll have is mother-in-law trouble."

Arthur had a mind of his own so in two years he had a cute little wife whose name was Amarilla Ant. So later on poor Arthur had a family, a wife and two kids. Their names were Ann and Andy.

But beside all this Arthur needed a job. Amarilla said for him to go over to the shoe store.

"But be sure to put shoes on men only." Amarilla was a very jealous ant.

Mr. Brown, the ant that owned the store, let Arthur have the job. But one day Amarilla caught Arthur putting a shoe on a lady. Poor Arthur! Next thing he knew he had a broken arm, a bashed-in head, and two black eyes and was in the Antville Sickhouse.

After two months in the Antville Sickhouse, he went home to find that his wife had gone home to her mother and had left the children home.

CHAPTER TWO: *Mother-in-Law Trouble*

That night SHE came home with her mother! ! ! Ann and Andy ran up to greet her but Arthur ran and hid. Lucky the kids didn't see him! They were such tattle tales. Arthur was planning to jump out and say, "Boo!"

"Where's Arthur?" said Amarilla.

"He was in the living room last we knew," said Ann.

"And looking mighty sad at that," said Andy.

Well, as you see, with Arthur hiding and Amarilla bringing her mother home, Arthur was in for an awful mess. As Amarilla came down the hall with her mother, they were just about to pass Arthur's hiding place, when Arthur remembered that Amarilla's mother had heart trouble. So he came out of his hiding place very slowly and very softly he said, "H-h-hi."

"Oh, so THERE YOU ARE!" yelled Amarilla. "You goon! Why weren't you at the door when we came home, you goon? You drip! Don't you say a word until I'm finished. Blah, blah, blah." And before Arthur could say a word he had two black eyes and a broken arm and a bashed-in head and besides all that he was in the Antville Sickhouse again.

THE END

P. S. Arthur told me to tell you that when he gets out of the sickhouse he's going to go back to Harvard.

A fourth-grade girl

Nig's Not the Only Toughie

The five bears were playing checkers on their father's red and black fishing jacket. All of a sudden there was such a big roar you would think it was all the earthquakes in the world put together. Suddenly Paddy, their father, came barging into the room with his fishing pole in his hands. In a few minutes there was a broken fishing pole and five sore seats.

The next day Miss Grump, their teacher, told the children to put their tables in test position for a reading study hall. After ten minutes the teacher got discouraged at the five bears and said, "SIT DOWN, for heaven sakes."

The five bears said all together, "We can't."

"Why not?" asked the teacher.

"Because we don't have anything to cover our seats with so they won't sting when we do," they said.

After school the five bears went down to the penny bubble gum store where they were to meet rich Aunt Ethel and her very naughty boy named Brownie.

"I ain't gonna go," said Nig.

"Why not?" said Mo.

"Dat kid is gonna break my record," said Nig.

"How?" asked Eenie.

"He's tougher'n me!" said Nig.

At the penny bubble gum store we find four bears screaming with laughter while we find one bear screaming with pains from the seventy hundred millionth hair on his head to the last fraction of an inch on his toe nails.

Later we find out why Nig didn't want to meet his cousin. Nig was crying because a tornado had just hit his room. Brownie, his tough cousin, had beaten him up. Now Nig knew just what Mo hated.

THE END

A fourth-grade girl

"Aw gee wiz, Ma," said Nig, "every night we have to go through the worst treatment there is."

"Yeah," said Mo. Then the rest of the chorus joined in — that is Eenie, Meenie, and Meinie.

"Taking a bath? O, you don't really mind it," said Mother Bear. "I can see it in your little innocent faces. Now get along and don't forget the three rules: 1. Warm bath water. 2. No splashing. 3. Wash behind the ears."

"Holy cow," said Nig as he lead the others up the stairs. "First it was every three nights. Then it was every other night. Now it's every night. I wish Pop would get home from that fishing trip. He's been gone at least two weeks now. Maybe he'd put a stop to a bath every night."

"I doubt it," said Meenie. "He usually always agrees with Ma."

"Well, you guys, we can always hope. Hurry! Maybe we can get finished in time to listen to The Lone Bear."

Five minutes later: "Hand over the wash cloth. Ouch, wa-a-a. I got soap in my eyes. This water is sure hot enough."

Still later: "Come on! Get him, get the bad guy! Gee, the Lone Bear sure is tricky."

"Time to go to bed, children," said Mother Bear.

"But, Mom, the program's not finished yet."

"Well, it almost is nine — pretty late for little bears like you."

"But, Mom —— "

"No *buts* or *ands*."

Golly, just then Father came in the door. "Oh, darling, I am so glad to see you." (Smack smack.)

"The children are being a nuisance," said Mother.

"I'll put a stop to that."

A few minutes later. "When will these ice cubes be frozen?"

A fourth-grade girl

Nig's Trouble

One day Nig was playing outside when Molly Lou came by. Molly is always trying to kiss him ever since he saved her from the fire at Roy Bear's house.

"Oh, my hero," she said.

"Shut up," said Nig.

"Oh, oh!" said Molly Lou. "I guess you don't want any of my candy."

"Why, Molly Lou, I didn't mean it. I was only joking."

"O.K.," she whispered, "but you have to take me to the movies after I give it to you."

"Well — I — guess — so." (Then after Nig had finished.) "Oh, Molly Lou, I have to go in and take my music lesson."

"But — but — "

Just then with a flash of lightning Nig was gone. Nig sneaked out of the kitchen.

"Oh, no, you don't! You're going to take your music lesson," said Molly Lou. And the last time I saw Nig he was taking his music lesson and Molly Lou was singing for him. This is the song she was singing: Oh, My Love, Nig.

A fourth-grade girl

One day (his room looked very gloomy) Joey Bear said to Moey Bear, "Let's go swimming."

"But Mommy said —— "

"Aw 'fraid cat! I don't care what she said. I'm going to swim."

"Oh, you are, are you?" said Mother Bear as she walked in the door.

Two minutes later Joey Bear was wishing he hadn't talked to Moey. Then he had a bright idea (he thought). He went into his closet, rummaged around in the junk until he found the rope to his cowboy suit. Then he tied it to the radiator just inside the window. He let down the rope very carefully. Then he made sure the knot was tight enough. He looked down. Suddenly it looked very far to the ground but he just had to do it. He was half way down the rope when there was a distinguished squeak from the front door. Joey saw to his horror that it was Aunt Brown Bear. He moved very fast. As he went past the hall window he saw something which made him panic stricken because he saw Mother Bear *going into his room!* And a few strands of the old rope were broken and he was slipping.

Just then the last of the rope gave way and he fell right on his aunt's new porcupine quill hat. "Yow-ow-ow! My seat! Ow-ow! Jeepers, it hurts. I give up," Joey cried.

Mother Bear came out. "I am going to give you something you deserve," she said.

"No — no — not the hair brush?"

"No, you've learned your lesson. I'm going to give you a new cowboy rope."

THE END

A fourth-grade boy

Letters Can Mean Trouble

One day a letter came for Mo. It was from one of Mo's girl friends. She said:

DEAR MO,

Can you come to my party?
It is a dress up party and
since you are a boy you will
have to dress up like a girl.

Love,

BETTY BEAR

Mo was so excited he put the letter in his mother's top drawer but Nig happened to find the letter. And the next day Nig put it up on the bulletin board in his classroom so all the kids could see it.

When Mo came in, all the bears laughed at him — even the teacher. Mo was so embarrassed.

After school he put a mouse trap in Nig's chair and when Nig sat down to supper there were a few screams and yells that could only come from a brat named Nig.

THE END

A fourth-grade girl

Wash Day *

"Children," said Mother Bear, "today is Monday and a holiday from school — and *now*," she said in a low tone with a little gleam in her eye, "you can do some washing. Wash day, you know — YOUR WASH DAY."

The five bears slowly, inch by inch, got up from the dinner table, but in the wink of an eye Mother Bear caught them by their big floppy ears and dropped them one by one ker spash into the tub.

A fifth-grade boy

"Children, I have a treat for you," said Miss Flower, the bear's teacher, "a special treat."

"What is it?" asked the class in chorus. "Is it ice cream and cake?"

"Oh no, much better than that," said the teacher. "Miss Brown — she is one of the teachers in a western university — she has come to see how boys and girls act."

Miss Brown smiled and began to speak. "I love to come and visit schools and see the boys and girls. You remind me of my childhood. I teach older boys and girls, but they are almost grown up while you are just beginning life. How I envy Miss Flower, your beloved teacher, for she has you with her every day."

Miss Flower was very jealous of Miss Brown, but she hid her own feeling and offered Miss Brown her chair. She didn't know that Nig had put a tack in the chair. Miss Brown sat down. Miss Brown got up rather fast and started for the door.

"I never did like children," she said as she started through the door.

"You shouldn't have done that, children," said Miss Flower, but she gave them each ten cents to buy a Good Humor with.

A fifth-grade girl

The Porkville Army

"Left, left, halt." There was a moment of confusion and the Porkville Army came to a halt.

"Now we'll have roll call," said Tit, who was the general. "Ezra Squirrel?"

"Here."

"Tat?"

"Here."

---

* This is the first story written by a new fifth-grade boy.

"Toe?" There was no answer. "Well, what are you waitng for?" shouted Tit. "Go and find him."

In a minute the whole of Porkville was in a hubbub, but Toe couldn't be found. After the army got reassembled Tit screamed, "Well, where is he?" Then he sent them off a second time and retired to his tent.

Very soon a little pink head appeared from behind a crate of turnips and quickly disappeared again as a mud ball hit the wall above him. When the army got to the crate there was nothing but a hole in the turnip crate and a lot of footprints. Meanwhile the body that owned the little pink head was running hastily to the Porkville Army headquarters, where Tit sat lazily chewing a stick of molasses candy. The little pink head and body, in other words Toe, began quietly to cut a hole in the back of the tent. A minute later when Tit reached down to the molasses box he couldn't find anything . Two minutes later he was struggling to get out of a fallen-down tent.

"Let me out of here. Help. Splutter," he mumbled.

A peal of laughter came from outside the tent, but shortly it turned into angry squeals for the Porkville Army had come back.

* * *

"Livingston, I presume," said Nig as he entered Tit's tent.

"Yeah," said Tit, kicking Nig into the empty molasses box.

"Whee," said Nig as he went whizzing through the air, "now for a three-point landing."

Crash! Nig had got stuck in the molasses box. "Blubbity blub" was the only thing Tit could hear. Then Nig shouted, "Let me out of here! Why, I'll sue you for this."

"All right. I challenge you warmly. You can go home now," said Tit to Nig, whose head was still stuck in the molasses box.

* * *

Next morning Tit and his army were getting ready for the fight with wooden swords and mud balls. Then Tit gave his last orders and saw that Toe was well guarded. Just then over the hillcrest came Nig and his twenty Rough Riders, and with this army came marching a flag. From the flag came a voice saying, "But, Nig — "

"Shut up!" came the reply. But Mo, who was the flag bearer could not finish his sentence because a mud ball found its mark.

"Men," said Nig, "there is the enemy. Are you scared of a little mud? Why look at me. I'm facing —— "

Spleosh, oo, blub, splutter.

After wiping the mud off his face Nig, under a small cloud of swearing, began his speech again. With a big, confident smile he said, "Everybody who's with me say 'yah'."

A hushed silence came over the army of bears huddled closely together. Nig's smile became almost invisible. Then he shouted. "Charge!"

Alone he rushed forward. Before he could do anything the army of pigs was upon him. There was a splash, a splosh, and a hollow-sounding bong as a wooden sword hit a bear's head.

The bears did not wait to see what happened to their general, Nig, but retreated with the flag straggling after. There was a gust of wind as Nig passed them, doing what he called "covering the retreat."

A fifth-grade boy

The five little bears were in school one afternoon. "Now," said the teacher," I will tell you something. On your way home will you hunt for signs of spring?"

Nig shot a bean out of his beanshooter.

"Ouch! Oh-h-h-!" said the teacher.

"That's a sign of spring," said Nig.

"You're dismissed," the teacher said.

"Good!" said all the bears except Mo.

The next day the bears went to school bright and early. But Nig decided to play hooky. He sneaked away from the other bears.

"I hope," said Mo, "that we won't be late."

"Come on. Let's run or we will be," said the other bears.

When they got to school the teacher asked if they had seen any signs of spring. Meenie raised his hand and said, "I was digging and I found a worm and it was growing pink."

"No, Meenie-a-I-er-a don't think that's a very good sign of spring," said the teacher.

"You don't say so," said Meenie. "Why, where is Nig?"

The teacher said surprised, "Huh?"

The bears said, "I guess he must have played hooky, don't you?"

"Yes I do," said the teacher. "Eenie, Meenie, Meinie, and Mo, go out and find Nig."

"All right," they said. They went out doors and saw a truck.

"I'll tell you what let's do," Eenie said. "Let's get up in the truck and ride all over town and maybe we will find Nig."

"I see," the other bears said.

They got up in the truck and lay down as flat as they could. Mo whimpered a little after they were on the way. "Oh, stop your crying and look," said Eenie.

They finally saw a little ash can walking around on two brown, fat, chubby bear legs.

"I think that I see Nig," said Eenie.

"Where?" the other bears said.

"Over there," he pointed to the ash can.

The bears tumbled out of the truck. "Oh dear — oh dear — oh dear!" they said. They ran over to Nig. "Hey, you've got to go home."

They pulled off the ash can. Nig did not want to go home. The four little bears pulled and pulled. They got Nig home. About an hour later Nig was rubbing his seat. The other little bears were eating a nice piece of cherry pie. "Um-m-m — " they were saying when they got to bed.

A fifth-grade boy

Mo's New Coat

"Nig," called Mother Bear, "come here and bring Mo."

In came Nig, dragging Mo by the ear, but he let go when he saw Mother Bear, and held him gently by the hand.

"Why are you crying so, Mo dear?" asked Mother Bear.

"Oh," said Mo, sniffling and holding his ear," " — er — " Just then he saw Nig with his fist in fighting form. " — er, nothing, Mother."

"Well, I want you, Nig," said Mother Bear, raising her voice for she saw Nig sticking his finger in the sugar bowl.

Nig turned around and started twiddling his sticky thumbs angelically. "Yes, Mother," he said.

"I want you," repeated Mother Bear, "to go with Mo and get him a new coat. Be sure to see that it fits well. I'm too busy to go. Please be back quickly," she added, jerking Nig's finger out of the sugar bowl again. "And charge it." she said, pushing them out. "Good-by. Oh, if there ever was the likes of them. Whew!"

Meanwhile at the store Nig was trying coats on Mo. He took the biggest one. "This will fit you nicely, Mo darling," he said, and he wrapped it on Mo. He told the man their address and left.

"But, Niggy dear," said Mo, "It's too big. Mother said I should have a size thirteen and you've got size forty."

"Aren't you satisfied?" said Nig, showing his fist.

"Why — er — yes, Niggy, I am," said Mo trembling. "Y-y-yes, sh-sh-sure I a-am."

"Come on then," said Nig roughly. "We'll never get home if you don't hurry."

Ding, ding.

"Why, hello, Nig," said Mother, Where's Mo?"

"There," said Nig, pointing to a large coat with two legs sticking out. "There he is."

"Oh," said Mother sternly, "is that Mo's new coat?"

"Yes," said Nig backing away, "that's Mo's new coat."

"Well, young bear," said Mother, taking Nig over her knee, "you can march right back to the store and get the coat changed, and no allowance for you this week."

Five minutes later a bedraggled bear started off in the direction of the coat store, holding a coat and his seat.

A fifth-grade girl

Nig Shows Off Daisy May

The bears were coming home from school. Nig was running so fast that the other bears had a hard time keeping up with him. Now this was very unusual for Nig, for he always dallied on the way, stopping at the baseball field to bat a few balls. But today he hurried; no one knew why. But Eenie suspected that he had a date with Susie Bear.

When they got home Nig ran up to Mother Bear's room. The other bears followed him because they wanted to know where he was going. When they got up to the room Nig was talking breathlessly.

"There's a new girl in school called Elizabeth Ann, and I am going over to see her this afternoon, and bring Daisy May for she wants me to."

"Well, all right," said Mother Bear. "Wrap her up warmly in a blanket, and you will have to dress her."

"So he is going over to see Elizabeth Ann," thought Mo, "and show her Daisy May, and I wanted to. Well, I'll fix him." Then Mo said in a very sweet voice, "Let me dress her for you."

"Oh, all right. Put on her best dress and her best coat and hat and put her in her new carriage and put on her new blanket."

With these instructions Nig straightened his tie and combed his hair while Mo went to fix Daisy May. Ten minutes later Mo wheeled Daisy May's carriage into the living room where Nig was.

"Don't pull the hood up," said Mo, "for she is asleep."

"All right," said Nig. Taking the handle of the carriage in one hand and his father's cane in the other he started over to Elizabeth's. When he got there Elizabeth ran down to meet him.

"Oh, let me see Daisy May!"

"Why, Nig, you deceitful thing. Don't you think I can tell the difference between a person and a doll? You are teasing, you mean thing!" With that she went into the house and Nig was left with the doll.

That night at supper Mo had a black eye and Nig had a warm seat.

A fifth-grade boy

The Five Bears Start an Orchestra

One day the five bears decided to start an orchestra. Mo was to play the drum. He couldn't quite reach the top, but he had talent. They discovered it one time when Nig was fighting Mo and Mo started pounding on his back. Meinie played the tuba. He did it 'cause it hid him and if he struck a sour note, nobody would know who did it. Meenie played the flute 'cause he knew Joy Bear was coming, and she could see him easily with the flute. Eenie played the violin. When he was small he had swallowed a toy whistle; so he said he wouldn't mind the squeaks. Nig had the bass violin 'cause he liked to take up a lot of room to be noticed.

One day their school decided to put on an amateur hour, and the bears decided to enter their orchestra. Finally the great day arrived and they were very much excited. They just got there in time.

"Ladies and gentlemen, and contestants, we present to you tonight Major Blows, who is to judge our contest. The first contestants are Ecnie, Mcenie, Meinie, Mo, and Nig Bear, who have an orchestra."

They all took their places and began. Mo and Nig started a piece called "Thunder," while the rest played a piece called "Twinkling Stars." The discord was enough to blow everybody out of the auditorium. They finally finished quickly and took their seats. At the end everyone was supposed to clap for the best, but when the orchestra went on the stage, nobody made a sound.

"Aw gee," said Nig, "nobody appreciates good music."

A fifth-grade girl

Tall, Middle-Size, and Small

Once upon a time in a little house lived three otters. They lived with their mother and father (of course). The tallest otter's name was Tall; the middle-sized otter's name was Middle-Size; the little wee otter's name was — What do you think it was? — Small!

One day Tall, Middle-Size, and Small said to their mother, "Mother," said Tall.

"Mother," said Middle-Size.

"Mama," said Small in his small wee voice.

"Mother," they said all together, "Mother, we are going to do something, but we can't think what it is. What are we going to do?" they asked.

"Why, don't you know? You are going to the fair with your father and me."

"Oh, yes, yes, yes! Now we know," they cried.

"Now we know! Now we know! Now we know!" repeated Small.

"Oh, shut up," said Tall, "or it will be the worse for you." Small began to whimper but brightened up at the promise of an ice cream from his mother.

"You spoil him," said Tall who was just like his father.

"What's that about spoiling somebody?" came a cheery voice.

"Oh, nothing," said Tall grumpily. "She's just spoiling Small just 'cause he's the littlest."

"Well, Oscar, after all he IS the littlest and —— " said Mrs. Otter.

"I know, Ophelia," said Mr. Otter, "but you shouldn't baby him."

"Well, why shouldn't I? After all, he's our smallest child — "

"Well, why don't you do something about it? Why don't you give birth to another baby otter? That's an idea!"

"That's an idea! I'll do it. I'll have another baby."

"She'll have another baby," echoed Small.

"Oh, hush up," said Tall.

CHAPTER TWO: *The Baby's Arrival*

When it came, it was a girl and on the day of its arrival the mother called the children into her room. When all were assembled (even the father), the mother said, "Now children, what shall we call the baby?" Silence. . . . "Well?"

"We're thinking." More silence. . . .

Then from Tall, "We could call it Ophelia after you, Mother."

"And call her Ophy for short," put in Middle-Size and then he giggled. "Can you tell why?"

Then Small said, "We could call her Small Junior after *me.*"

"Who would want to name anything after *you?* You're the smallest." Tall is speaking.

"I'm the smallest," echoed Small regretfully.

But then Mother said, "Not any more, sugar plum. That little girl in the cradle is the smallest *now.* But come, can't anybody think of a better name than Ophelia or Small Junior? Papa, can you think of anything?"

"Why not call her Tiny? That's a good name."

"Yes, yes," said everybody, "let's call her Tiny."

"Let's call her Tiny," echoed Small but nobody said, "Hush up," this time.

CHAPTER THREE: *Going to the Fair*

Going to the fair had to be delayed a few weeks 'til the baby should be able to sit up in the baby carriage. But animals grow very fast and Tiny was no exception. So in a few weeks Tiny could walk, a little wobbly perhaps, but still she could walk.

So one sunny morning they started out for the fair. As soon as Tiny was tired, Mr. Otter picked her up and carried her. It was plain that Tiny was Mr. Otter's favorite for nobody likes to have all boys however nice they may be. After all, one likes to have at least one of a different sex.

Finally they reached the fair-grounds. Small shrieked with delight when he saw the ferris wheel. Tall and Middle-Size acted more grown-up than Small but they were pleased never-the-less. Tiny could not go on the ferris wheel as she was still a baby but she did not seem to know what she was missing and gurgled and cooed all the time.

When Tall, Middle-Size, and Small came down from the ferris wheel, they all went to the merry-go-round. Small and Tiny wanted to try it immediately but Tall and Middle Size said, "Ach, such babies to ride on a merry-go-round."

But Small and Tiny didn't mind. Indeed, Tiny *could* not understand a word they said as she was only a few weeks old.

All afternoon they gorged themselves on hot dogs and soda pop and ice creams — that is, all except Tiny. *Her* diet was limited to one ice cream and a glass of orange juice.

What a happy afternoon they had! And when it was all over and they were riding home in the wagon, Small said, "Gee, we had fun!"

THE END

A fifth-grade girl

Small Gets a Haircut

"Why does everything have to happen to me?" Small sighed. "Huh! I don't need a haircut anyway. Women are so silly, always thinking little boys need haircuts. Well, here I am. Should I go in or should I stay out? Oh, I might as well go in — but — Oh, I'll go in."

He walked slowly into George Goat's barbershop. "I want a crow-cut," he announced.

"Don't you mean a crew-cut?" asked the attendant.

"No," said Small, "I mean a crow-cut. Just like the crows wear."

The attendant finally got Small settled in the barber's chair. "Now you say you want a crew-cut," he began.

"A crow-cut," said Small firmly.

"But — but there isn't any such thing as a crow-cut," said the bewildered attendant.

"I don't care," said Small; "I want one anyway."

The attendant said he'd try and was just about to put the sheet about Small's neck when Small suddenly said, "I don't need a bib. Watcha putting a bib on me for?"

The attendant's pride was hurt. "Young man," he said sternly, "this is not a bib. It is merely a sheet to keep the hair off your clean suit — "

"Tain't clean," said Small sullenly.

"So you won't get it dirty," continued the attendant.

"Don't care if I do get it dirty," pouted Small.

"Now *will* you sit still?" asked the attendant impatiently, after a vain attempt to cut Small's hair straight.

"Why?" asked Small impishly.

"Because," said the attendant, "if you don't I won't be able to cut your hair straight and then you won't look nice."

"Don't wanna look nice," said Small. "Wanna go home."

"Go home then," said the angry attendant.

"All right, I will," and Small stomped out of the barber shop, the soap suds all over his head.

A fifth-grade boy

The Five Bears Go Daisy Picking

"Oh gee," said Mo, "I wish there was something to do."

"You can come and look at the postman with me," said Nig, who was perched in the window and staring at the postman. "He's coming up our front walk now."

Ding, ding. The doorbell rang.

"I hope he has something for us," said Eenie as he ran over to the door.

"Yere's a letter for ye boys," said the postman as he busily chewed his tobacco.

"Looks like it's from Sue Bear's house. Hey, look, it's an invitation to a-a-aoh-h — ." Eenie collapsed.

"Read it, Nig," said Mo excitedly. "What's it say?"

"We're invited to a — oh, my gosh — to a daisy-picking party."

"Oh-h," they all moaned, "I've got a stomach ache," and they all dashed upstairs, that is all but Mo. He stopped to look at the invitation.

"Golly, of all the stupid things to ask he-men like us to go to. I — Gee, what's this? Refreshments will be served. Golly, I'm going."

CHAPTER TWO

"Now children," warned Mrs. Bear, "don't go near the railroad tracks."

"We won't," and then they all started picking. After about half an hour Mo spied a wonderful, big daisy a few inches away from the tracks. He quickly ran over and looked down the tracks. Then he stooped over. A train from the other direction came speeding down, and the cow-catcher caught Mo right in the seat of his pants.

"E-e-e-e-K," squeaked Sue, "Mo's cowed on the caught-catcher — I mean catched on the cow-caught — I mean — E-e-ek! Look!"

As Mrs. Bear turned she just saw a quick glance of Mo speeding around the corner.

CHAPTER THREE

It was a peaceful day for the three bulls in Farmer Brown's field as they stood there munching grass. Soon the four o'clock train came roaring down the tracks. They all stopped and looked. Suddenly a brown and red thing flew off and landed a few feet from them. (Mo's best suit was bright red.)

"RED!" they roared and went flying towards poor Mo.

"Ah-h," he thought, "there's a place I can get through."

He started running, but there before him loomed the biggest person he had ever seen. It was Farmer Brown's daughter, who was known all over the country for her bigness and also her affection.

"Oh, oo toot wittle fing," she cried, "is oo wunning fom da big, naughty bulls?" And she stood there with her arms out waiting to clasp Mo.

"Oh, golly," said Mo, "I'm stuck."

An unfinished story written by
a sixth-grade boy.

Eau de Cologne

"One more tack," said Nig to Mo. "When we get this sign up our
luck begins."

Nig was pasting a sign on the door. It read:

CLASSICAL BEAUTY PARLOR

MUD PACKS   HAND PERMANENTS
                MANICURES
HAIR CUTS   BACK MASSAGE

CHILDREN ONLY 3¢ TO 13¢

The five bears had decided that they would have a beauty parlor
and get rich. They had fixed up the attic. In it was a bucket of
mud, a bucket full of water, four chairs, Eenie's toy cash register
bank, which was on top of the book case which had three or four
Mickey Mouse magazines on it, a copy of Red Riding Hood,
Grimm's Fairy Tales with three pages out, a funny page from the
Saturday paper, a Big-Little book, and a cupboard, which contained
miscellaneous things such as water paints and bobby pins. The last
had come from Mother's room, and there was a table with a vase
on which had some withered daisies which Mo had contributed.
The beauty specialists were in the attic when the bell rang. Nig
opened it with a bow. There stood Ann Bear.

"Are you the manager of the beauty parlor?" she said.

"Yes," said Nig, guessing that he was.

"Well," said Ann Bear, "I want a mud pack, please. Where shall
I go?"

"Er — uh right upstairs. Follow me," said Nig. "Here we are,"
he said as they came to the attic. "Sit right down, please. Hey,
Meenie, how do you give a mud pack anyhow?"

"I don't know," answered Meenie.

"Well, I guess you just put mud on a person's face. Yeah — well
here I go. Now, Madam," said Nig, "please sit back."

He picked up a rag, dipped it in the mud, and washed Ann's face
with it.

"There," said Nig. "Four cents please."

"But you're not finished," said Ann Bear, "you have to wash
it off."

"Why," said Nig, "our sign didn't say so. It says MUD PACKS.
It didn't say a thing about washing it off, but since you're so un-
happy about it I will take it off for one cent."

"Oh, all right," said Ann, who had been wondering what she

was going to do. Nig got another rag, dipped it in the water, and washed it off. Nig thought it was a perfect job, but he did not see how Ann's yellow fur was still striped with brown.

"Well," said Ann, "here's your five cents. Good-bye."

As soon as Ann had gone Eenie said, "Nig, it's my turn now."

"O.K.," said Nig, "you can take care of the next customer, but," he warned, "do it good."

Eenie had just mumbled something under his breath about he wasn't so hot when the door bell rang. Eenie slid down the bannisters and opened the door. "Why," he said, "it's Louise Bear."

"Yes," said Louise Bear, "I have come to have a hand permanent."

"O.K.," said Eenie; "follow me."

"All right," said Louise Bear.

"Er," said Eenie as they got up to the attic, "would you pay me in advance, please?"

"I suppose so," said Louise Bear, "how much?"

"Three cents," said Eenie, "for the rubber bands, two cents for the trouble, one cent for doing it. That adds up to um — er — let me see — three cents and two cents make five cents plus two cents more makes seven cents exactly."

"Very well," said Louise Bear, "where shall I sit?"

"Over there," said Eenie, thinking that the water pail was a chair.

Louise Bear sat down. "Oh," she cried, "my new dress! Give me back my money!"

"Now, now," said Eenie, "you know it was just a mistake." "Wasn't," yelled Louise Bear. "I'm going to tell my mummy." And she ran home.

"You're not so good," said Mo timidly. "Let me try."

"Oh, all right. See what you can do," said Eenie.

"Oh, goody," said Mo. "Just watch me."

Just then Mother Bear, who did not know what the bears were doing, led the real estate man upstairs to the attic. He had come to see about repairs and Mother was saying to him, "And the attic needs repainting."

She opened the door of the attic.

"So," said the real estate man, "this is the way you take care of your house. The company shall hear of this." And the man started to go out the door.

"Wait, Sir," said Mo. "Would you like a hair cut?"

"How much?" said the man.

"Three cents, Sir," said Mo.

"O.K. Clip away," said the real estate man softening.

Mother Bear was so grateful to Mo for saving the day that she called up the drug store and ordered five chocolate ice cream cones for the bears. Meanwhile Mo started cutting. Cut-cut, cut, cut.

"Are you finished?" said the man after a while when Mo stopped.

"Yes," said Mo, innocently, "there isn't a hair left on you."

"What?" yelled the man.

"I said," said Mo, "that there's not a hair left on you by this time."

Mo Bear, Eenie, Meenie, Meinie, and Nig were laughing so hard they were crying.

"Well," said the man cooling off, "since you are so sorry I shall not report this."

That night Mother Bear was so mad about the attic not being painted that she took the five bears to the drug store and got them five sodas each.

A sixth-grade boy

There was a big sign on the Bear's front door marked, QUARANTINE. The word was written in big red letters, and underneath the big letters was written in small black type *No one is to enter this house for Mo Bear has scarlet fever.*

"Look at the sign Mo got Mother to put up," said Nig.

The little bears were just coming home from school — that is all but Mo, for he had not felt very well that morning and Mother had made him stay in bed.

"What sign?" asked the little bears in chorus.

"This sign saying he has got the scarlet fever. He's jealous 'cause we're having our girls over this afternoon to see Daisy May and he can't have his," and with that Nig tore up the sign in little bits. He gave the pieces to Meenie, who liked jigsaw puzzles so much that he was always doing them, and when he didn't have any to do he put little pieces of paper together.

Just then Dotty Bear and Sue and Judy and Doris Bear came along. "We have come to see Daisy May," they said.

"Come right in," said Nig. "We have been waiting for you." With that the little bears brought the girls into the house.

"Mother!" called Eenie, "the girls have come to see Daisy May."

"What!" said Mrs. Bear, coming to the landing. She was very white — that is as white as a brown bear can be. She was very worried. Who wouldn't be with a child sick with scarlet fever and a baby to take of, to say nothing of four other noisy children? And now she was going to have four little girls. That was the last straw. She was so upset that she sat down and cried. Just then the door opened and in came the doctor, who was purple with rage.

"Who took that sign off the door?" he said in a loud voice.

"We did," said the four bears in very weak voices.

"And why are those girls here?" asked the doctor, who didn't hear them.

"Oh, I don't know," cried Mother Bear.

"Well, never mind," said Dr. Pinkpill. "It isn't your fault. I am going up to see Mo."

Mother Bear followed Dr. Pinkpill up the stairs; so the bears were left alone with the little girls.

"I hate you, Nig! I am never going to speak to you again. I'll get scarlet fever and die. You mean, mean bear, how could you take that sign down?" and Sue Bear began to weep.

"I don't care," said Nig. "I'll become engaged to the new girl — Amelia."

"What?" asked Sue Bear. "Don't you love me?"

"Ye-es," said Nig slowly, "but Amelia's prettier."

"But if you love me and I love you it would be a shame to keep us apart."

"Yes, I suppose it would, but I thought you didn't love me."

Just then Mrs. Bear came down the stairs with Dr. Pinkpill. "But how could you make such a mistake?" asked Mrs. Bear.

"Well, anyone could do it," said Dr. Pinkpill. "In fact, no doctor knows the difference between scarlet fever and a food rash in the beginning. Here's the bill — $25.00 for two visits."

"What?" cried Mrs. Bear. "I won't pay you a cent. The idea of scaring me and these poor children!"

"Yes," said Dr. Pinkpill meekly, "of course I was only joking."

"You had better be," said Mother Bear.

A sixth-grade girl

The Love Story

The clock struck twelve. A silent figure slipped down the Five Bears' lane. It was carrying something that looked like a guitar. The figure was humming a love song. "Oh love, oh love," the figure was whispering.

Next morning came, Sunday morning. Mo found a note pinned to Nig's empty bed. It read:

"I have gone to sing a love song to Patricia Bear. If she refuses me, I don't think I shall ever come home. If she loves me I shall come home with her as my bride."

Mo giggled his silly little giggle. He knew that the letter had come out of the book of etiquette for the man in love.

"Father," Mo exclaimed, "Nig is in love."

Father Bear grunted sleepily. It wasn't news to him, but he got up and sloshed his feet into his heel-less slippers and scuffed down the hall to Nig's room.

At eight when the four bears and Daisy were eating breakfast there came a feeble knock at the door. In stepped Nig with two black eyes, and a very red ear, and he was limping. The once beautiful guitar was hanging around his neck.

"She has refused me," he broke out tragically.

"So I see," barked Father Bear unsympathetically.

"You'd better go to bed," said Mother Bear coldly. It was the only way she could think of to get rid of him.

"You, my dear Mo," Nig said, "may have the pleasure of taking Daisy May to Sunday School." Nig was still feeling romantic. Mo groaned. He knew what it was to take Daisy to Sunday School.

Finally the Four and Daisy were off. They had left Nig in bed, smelling terribly of liniment and reading *How to Win Your Love*. When they got to church Mo warned Daisy about how quiet she must be.

"Aw wight, Mo," she said.

When they got in Daisy went prancing up the aisle, saying hello to anyone she knew. Mo was so mad at her that he forgot himself and yelled at the top of his lungs, "You — you thing! Come here this instant."

Daisy turned slowly around. "Oh, Mosy," she squeaked, "you are in church. You mustn't yell." Then she put her fingers to her mouth. "Shush," she said, and turning she scrambled up the aisle to the front row and sat down.

Mo was so mad that he didn't know what to do. He started to let out one of his famous screams, but then a thought came to him. He stopped with his mouth open. He was in church. Mo blushed and blushed. Everyone was looking at him. Slowly he walked up the aisle, looking very silly with his hair going every which way and a face that looked like a tomato with hair. He grabbed Daisy May by one ear and scrambled to a seat. Then Sunday School started. He found himself beside Patricia Bear. Patricia Bear was feeling very sympathetic and good that morning after having beaten up Nig the night before.

"She — she isn't very good, is she?" she whispered, nodding at Daisy.

"Oh," said Mo, a little upset, "why, yes. No." he added giving innocent Daisy a kick.

Everything was all right till the plate was passed. Mo was so nervous that he still shook, and in reaching for the plate he gave a jerk and dropped it. Crash, bang! Money bounced everywhere. Everybody started scrambling for it. Mo thought he had come to the end and would die presently. He made one last effort.

"Patricia," he said above the noise, "make up with Nig for my sake. Please, please. He can take care of Daisy, he can."

"Oh," said Patricia, grabbing a quarter on the roll, "I have. I called him up this morning."

Mo, who was Mother's pet and not used to any strain, quietly fainted. From then on Daisy May had more respect for Mo.

"My bruvver can faint," she would say proudly.

Mo was proud of her, too. "My sister can make more trouble than a thousand bandits."

Nig never had any quarrel after that about taking Daisy May out.

A sixth-grade girl

Bibliography

Arnstein, Flora J., *Adventure Into Poetry*. San Francisco: Stanford University Press, 1951.

Baruch, Dorothy Walter, *Parents and Children Go To School*. Chicago: Scott Foresman and Co., 1939.

Betzner, Jean, *Content and Form of Original Compositions Dictated by Children Five to Eight Years Old*. New York: Teachers College, Columbia University, 1930.

Burrows, Alvina Treut, "Children's Writing and Children's Growth," *Elementary English*, XXVIII (April, 1951), pp. 205-210.

——, *Teaching Children in the Middle Grades*. Boston: D. C. Heath & Company, 1952.

——, "Writing As Therapy," *Elementary English*, XXIX (March, 1952), pp. 135-138, 149.

Cole, Natalie Robinson, *Arts in the Classroom*. New York: The John Day Company, Inc., 1940.

——, "Creative Writing as Therapy," *Elementary English Review*, XX (January, 1943), pp. 1-6.

234

Dawson, Mildred, "Guiding Writing Activities," *Elementary English Review,* XXIII (February, 1946), pp. 80-83, 97.

De La Mare, Walter, *Early One Morning in Spring.* New York: The Macmillan Company, 1935.

Dewey, John, *How We Think.* Boston: D. C. Heath & Company, 1933.

Dimnet, Ernest, *Art of Thinking.* New York: Simon & Schuster, Inc., 1929.

Downey, June, *Creative Imagination,* New York: Harcourt, Brace & Company, Inc., 1929.

Ferebee, June D., "Form through Creative Expression," *Elementary English,* XXVII (February, 1950), pp. 73-78.

———, "Gaining Power Through Writing," *Elementary English Review,* XIX (December, 1942), pp. 282-285.

Ferebee, June D., "Increasing the Writing Productivity in Children," University of Pennsylvania Bulletin, *36th Annual Schoolmen's Week Proceedings,* Philadelphia, Pennsylvania (March 30-April 2, 1949), pp. 47-53.

———, "What is Important in the Language Arts?" University of Pennsylvania Bulletin, *36th Annual Schoolmen's Week Proceedings,* Philadelphia, Pennsylvania (March 30-April 2, 1949), pp. 26-30.

———, and Jackson, Doris C., "Working with Children in Creative Writing," *Journal of the Childhood Education Association,* XVII, No. 6 (February, 1941), pp. 258-262.

Flesch, Rudolph, *The Art of Readable Writing.* New York: Harper and Brothers, 1949.

Hall, Robert A. Jr., *Leave Your Language Alone.* Ithaca, New York: Linguistica Publishers, 1950.

Henri, Robert, *The Art Spirit.* Philadelphia: J. B. Lippincott Company, 1939.

Jackson, Doris C., "Poetry Making With Children," *Elementary English Review,* XX (April, 1943), pp. 129-134.

La Brant, Lou, *Study of Certain Language Developments in Children in Grades IV-XII,* Clark University Press (Worcester: Journal Press, Provincetown), 1933.

———, *We Teach English.* New York: Harcourt, Brace & Company, Inc., 1951.

Mearns, Hughes, *Creative Youth.* Garden City, New York: Doubleday & Company, Inc., 1929.

National Council of Teachers of English, "Children Learn to Write," *Bulletin No. 7,* Fannie J. Ragland, Editor.

Perrine, V. D., *Let the Child Draw*. New York: Frederick A. Stokes Company, 1936.

Schmidt, Bernardine G., "Creative Ways of Retarded Children," *Elementary English*, XX (January, 1943), pp. 16-19.

Smith, Dora V., "Growth in Language Power as Related to Child Development," *Teaching Language in the Elementary School*, 43rd Yearbook of National Society for the Study of Education, Part II (Chicago: University of Chicago Press, 1944).

Smith, Ethel E., *Procedures for Encouraging Creative Writing in the Elementary School* (Ph.D. Thesis, Typewritten). Northwestern University School of Education, 1943.

Strickland, Ruth, *English is Our Language*, Guide for Teaching Grades I & II. Boston: D. C. Heath & Company, 1950.

———, *The Language Arts in the Elementary School*. Boston: D. C. Heath & Company, 1951.

Treut, Alvina, "Children's Creative Writing," *Arts in Childhood*, Bulletin No. 4, Series II, 6-9.

Watts, A. F., *The Language and Mental Development of Children*. Boston: D. C. Heath & Company, 1948.

Witty, Paul, "Creative Writing Climates," *Journal of the Childhood Education Association*, XVII No. 6 (February, 1941), pp. 253-257.

———, "Encouraging Growth and Development through Language Arts," *Arts in Childhood*, Bulletin No. 3, Series VI (1951), pp. 14-18.

———, "Opportunity to Write Freely," *Elementary English Review*, XIX (May, 1942), pp. 171-174.

Index

237